PARANORMAL
SUFFOLK

1. Scribbly Skull.

Paranormal Suffolk

True Ghost Stories

Christopher Reeve

Illustrated with line drawings by Mike Tingle

AMBERLEY

Dedicated to Martin Evans,

with thanks for all his help with the photographs.

First published 2009

Amberley Publishing Plc
Cirencester Road, Chalford,
Stroud, Gloucestershire, GL6 8PE

www.amberleybooks.com

Copyright © Christopher Reeve 2009

British Library Cataloguing in Publication Data.
A catalogue record for this book is available from the British Library.

ISBN 978 1 84868 375 4

Typesetting and Origination by Diagraf (www.diagraf.net)
Printed in Great Britain

CONTENTS

INTRODUCTION

I must begin by confessing that I've never seen a ghost. In fact, I tend to believe that I never will see one. I'm 'not that sort of person'. Yet, many people have said the same thing, and then been taken by surprise. The whole subject of the supernatural is mysterious and hard to explain, and it seems possible that anyone, at anytime, even the most die-hard sceptic, can suddenly encounter a phenomenon which defies and challenges our normal understanding of how the everyday world around us operates.

For most people, whatever their viewpoint, ghosts remain a fascinating topic. They generate a frisson of terror and excitement, and because they can never be entirely disproved, the 'Yes, but what if?' factor continues to dominate all our conversations about them. Shakespeare's most celebrated play *Hamlet* features a ghost, and every year dozens of new books, films and television programmes deal with ever more gory and elaborate stories connected with them. We laugh and joke about them with our families and friends, but – when walking home alone through a dark deserted churchyard, or sleeping alone in an old house when the door suddenly creaks open for no reason, or hearing a weird scream in the wind on a deserted coastal path – few of us could deny experiencing a quiver of fear that something horrible and strange might suddenly materialise in front of us.

The poet Coleridge's lines conjure up these sensations in what must surely be the most terrifying verse in the whole of English poetry:

> *Like one, that on a lonesome road*
> *Doth walk in fear and dread,*
> *And, having once turned round walks on,*
> *And turns no more his head;*
> *Because he knows, a frightful fiend*
> *Doth close behind him tread.*

Terrifying, because neither we, nor the traveller knows what will happen. He's been picked upon by a creature, so horrible, that he daren't even turn to face it; and from whom it seems he's powerless to escape.

Most books dealing with supernatural phenomena tend to include a wide variety of myths, legends and folklore, but *Paranormal Suffolk* focuses, as the sub-title suggests, principally on ghosts. By 'ghosts' I mean the souls or spirits of dead people which appear in some form or other to confront the living. They tend to haunt particular buildings or places associated with their mortal lives, and can potentially be seen by anybody who visits those spots. Ghostly apparitions can also include spectral beasts such as Black Shuck, strange creatures such as Freshwater Mermaids, and even phenomena such as phantom coaches, because although they are not manifestations of dead humans, they are all capable of being 'seen' by anybody who visits the places they inhabit.

This is not to imply that many people will see them. That depends entirely on the individual, and the circumstances. Some people seem to have a high degree of sensitivity to the paranormal, and children and animals are particularly receptive because their responses remain fresh and untrammelled by the weight of adult experience. Yet very few people seem to go through life without awareness of some form of haunting, even if only brief, and soon shrugged-off as 'weird' and unexplainable.

Interest in ghosts and the supernatural seems to occur in phases, and in the twenty-first century, there's a new surge of popularity, apparent to anybody going into a large bookstore and looking at the wide array of titles on the subject. This is somewhat surprising. It's easy to understand why our ancestors were gripped by the subject. They lived in times when there was little street lighting, and houses were lit only by flickering candles and the faint glow of firelight. Dark and shadowy places were bound to conjure up fears of the unexpected and unexplained. In addition, modern science now provides reasons for all sorts of occurrences in the natural world which puzzled previous generations. The eminent scholar, Dr Margaret Murray even claimed, in 1954, that 'Belief in ghosts, like belief in the devil, is dying out', and attributed it to the invention of electricity. Ghosts, she believed, can't exist where there's illumination.

So why is there a continued interest in spooks and spectres today? One reason is probably a reaction to what can seem the mundane nature of our everyday lives. Preoccupied with earning a living, our families, and domestic activities, we look for an escape beyond our normal sphere of existence, and the wide variety of supernatural subjects captures our attention. The decline in religious belief and regular attendance at places of worship, may also incline our thoughts more to the 'spirit' world, for which, Christianity and other religions have traditionally provided both an explanation, and a form of protection.

There may also be a connection with the way in which our lives are so much more comfortable than they were in past centuries. Modern technology, improved health and housing conditions, and the advances of medicine, can lull us into a sense of false security. Nothing, it seems, can harm us. But that's not the case. Life continues to be stressful, tragic, and painful to cope with. We are not invulnerable, and so at times, when we're alone, or frightened, or in unusual and perhaps threatening circumstances the same kind of feelings which caused our forbears to feel susceptible to unseen malevolent spirits can return to haunt us. Despite what scientists claim, much of life remains unexplained, and unexplainable; and so ghosts and demons will continue to inhabit the dark spaces of our minds and our environments.

This book, like most others on the subject, includes a large number of familiar ghost stories, handed down from one generation to another. As they get passed around, they can become embellished, and even associated with different circumstances from those in earlier versions. But that doesn't particularly matter. It's always been the method of oral tradition, and the important thing is that the core element remains convincing and authentic, and with the continuing capacity to surprise and alarm.

Apart from re-tellings of old Suffolk stories, these pages also contain new narratives, often connected with the town of Bungay in particular. Not just because it's my native town, I hasten to add, but because it's one of the most ancient, attractive and fascinating places in the whole of Suffolk. It's Roman and Saxon remains, Norman castle, mediaeval Priory, underground cellars and dungeons, and wealth of Tudor, Georgian, and Victorian buildings, has naturally attracted a long lineage of ghostly inhabitants who continue to astonish Bungay residents and visitors today.

And that's the point of this book. Ghosts remain perennially fascinating because you never know when you might be shocked by one. This book tells you about those who have been. Maybe, one day, your own story will be added.

FADING FOOTPRINTS
ROMAN AND SAXON SUFFOLK

The serene, low-lying countryside of Suffolk, with its scattered farms and hamlets, water meadows, and extensive coastline, seems an unlikely haunt for ghosts and demons. Such creatures are more often associated with dramatic landscapes, with the castles of the Rhineland and Transylvania, or the more elevated regions of Britain such as the Lake District and Scotland. Yet a motley array of ghostly spirits inhabit the region, some encountered throughout many centuries, others which come and go, and new ones appearing decade by decade.

So it seems that mountains, hills, caves, and grottoes are not necessary for ghosts to thrive. Perhaps they actually prefer a rural location like Suffolk, where there is plenty of space to expand their territory, and a wide choice of churchyards to haunt, Suffolk having more churches per square acre than almost any other county in England. Ghosts that favour this area include Black Dogs and other spectral beasts, phantom coaches, and headless horsemen, all of which seem to like drifting around, rather than being tied to one spot.

Wealthy land-owning lords have also contributed to the spirit population, by building castles or manor-houses where they can dwell, or provoking battles, quarrels and the spilling of blood, which attracts ghosts like carrion crows. In particular, the notorious Bigod family not only provided ideal locations for evil spirits, they often transmogrified into demons themselves after death so they could continue to persecute their neighbours and servants, just as they had done in life.

So, wherever you travel in Suffolk, you will never be far away from dim eyes glimmering at you from some gloomy hiding-place. Do you need to seek for them, or will they find you unsought? That's a question that's never been answered. Whether you're visiting a local church, or castle, or dining in a local pub, or even staying with a friend in an old thatched house, at any moment you could suddenly be experiencing the first ghostly encounter of your life. This book describes the many places where phantom spirits dwell, but there must be countless others that remain unrecorded, and perhaps a White Lady, a Saxon warrior, or a spectral Bogie Beast is just waiting for the opportunity to manifest itself in your presence. So 'Be Prepared', and don't let the opportunity slip away.

Apart from its varied character of farmland and coast, market towns and scattered villages, baronial halls, and dozens of fine flint-faced churches, Suffolk also has its very own 'House of Horrors'. Moyse's Hall is situated in Bury St Edmunds, and is

11

one of the earliest surviving dwelling-houses in the country. Now a museum, it's an excellent place to begin a tour of Haunted Suffolk, because it has its own special spooky character as well as a gruesome collection of exhibits that will wet your appetite for finding out more about their macabre associations.

As soon as you enter its door, you experience a tingle down your spine, for you are in a dark vaulted undercroft, with the spirits of thousands of previous long-dead inhabitants looming around you. Their presence is almost tangible, their murmurings almost audible, you expect at any moment to see a wispy white figure with his head under his arm drifting down the staircase towards you. It's quite a shock to turn and find a smiling assistant at the desk, welcoming you to the building, for she seems to have no place in this ancient dwelling of the dead.

Then you start to notice the exhibits displayed around the walls. The death mask of the murderer, William Corder, and a book bound in his own skin. An iron gibbet cage, in which hanged criminals were left to rot. Gruesome weapons of all sorts, cross-bows, swords and guns. Upstairs, witch-bottles containing human hair, urine and nails, to keep evil spirits at bay, mummified cats which have been incarcerated in chimney breasts, and many other objects connected with ghosts, demons, witches, and criminals, throughout the region's history. And all housed in one of the most atmospheric buildings you are ever likely to enter. Pause a while, as you walk around, to savour its unique atmosphere, the acrid taste of its history upon your lips: the sense that for this moment in time, time is suspended, and that you have become absorbed into another dimension – almost a ghost yourself?

So Moyse's Hall is the best place to get in the mind-frame to begin a tour of the county's haunted sites. And if you also go on to visit St Edmundsbury's other museum buildings at West Stow Village, you will discover extensive displays of Roman and Saxon objects which have been excavated in the surrounding area of West Suffolk. The very objects – urns, combs, knives, used everyday by the early inhabitants of the county, putting us literally 'in touch' with our past. Although most of the objects are reserved for display, others are made available for school-groups and other visitors to handle.

It's with these early settlers that this book commences. East Anglia, including Suffolk, was extensively populated by the invading Romans, followed by Saxon tribes, in the period before the Norman Conquest. It might therefore be expected that some of the ghosts haunting the region date from those centuries. If so, very few seem to survive. In *The Folklore of East Anglia*. Enid Porter refers to hauntings associated with prehistoric sites, and mentions the Shrieking Pits of Aylmerton, Norfolk, inhabited by ancient tribes, and haunted by a white screaming creature, and ghostly warriors that have been encountered at Hockwold Fen, also in Norfolk where a hoard of Roman silver was found. But these are only scanty examples, and none from Suffolk. In addition, the most recent and comprehensive account of national myths and legends, *The Lore of the Land* only mentions scanty hauntings throughout the whole of the country that relate to the Pre-Conquest period. But why should this be? Romans, Saxons, and other tribes were involved in violent incidents and savage battles, the land ran red with the blood of the slain, so surely some of the charismatic characters, and restless dead spirits should still be trying to communicate with us today.

The likely answer is that ghosts, unless they are particularly vibrant, troubled, and unappeased, eventually cease their hauntings, and depart in peace to the immortal world

2. Moyse's Hall Museum.

where all the other spirits of the dead find their final resting place. In other words they have a limited spell on earth even after death, and this may partly be because in life body and spirit are inseparable: therefore, once the body decays, the spirit formerly attached to it may grow weaker too, and eventually fade away altogether with the crumbling bones. In the mediaeval period it was believed that the spirits of the dead clung to their bodies for about a month after burial, so friends and relatives would keep a careful watch in the churchyard to remain in contact with their loved ones for as long as possible. And this belief still persists in some primitive cultures today.

So, if the spirit even of disturbed mortals only remains active for a limited period after death, those people living in the mediaeval period were more likely to see Roman and Saxon ghosts because they were closer to them in time. Similarly, Tudors were more likely to see mediaeval ghosts, and today we are more likely to encounter the disturbed dead of the Georgian and Victorian periods, and more recent burials. There will always be exceptions, and some spirits it seems, may be doomed to 'live again' throughout eternity, but that seems the most plausible explanation of why today, so few people can claim to be in touch with the really ancient dead.

An alternative reason could be that some of the spirits that hover un-quietly around us are not fully manifested. Therefore, it's impossible to know exactly what period of history they belong to. Also, ghosts are usually associated with particular buildings, or sites, so when those places decay or change and disappear the ghosts may vanish with

3. St Lawrence's Church, Ilketshall, beside the Roman road, Stone Street.

4. Roman god, on the porch of St Lawrence's church, Ilketshall.

them. Obviously most of the Roman and Saxon buildings of Britain are now vanished, and with no place to hide, their former ghostly occupants have vanished too. In Suffolk there are burial mounds, such as that at Eastlow Hill, near Rougham, the celebrated ship-burial at Sutton Hoo, the military fort at Burgh Castle, and the site of the Saxon village at West Stow, and many other interesting sites connected with early settlers, but not it seems, particularly connected with psychic phenomena.

If the ghosts of troubled spirits could indeed survive from all periods of time, we couldn't leave our houses at night, without running into great clouds of them everywhere, in the most irritating and inconvenient manner. It would be like walking out in a thick fog (– or could it be that fogs are partially formed of the wispy un-dead?) Ghosts, like everything else in nature have to be subject to the same eternal laws of change and decay. They must gradually fade away from further human communication, so we can all get a bit of peace.

The only significant Roman haunting recorded in *The Lore of the Land* is not too far from Suffolk, at the Strood on Mersea Island. There, a Roman centurion has been seen patrolling the area, usually on the night of the autumn equinox, around 23 September. Other ghostly figures are seen approaching him, and the clash of violent arms in combat can be heard. It is believed that a battle was fought near the spot, and a Roman grave with a burial urn and ashes was found nearby. So what is there about this particular site that it remains a Roman haunting place? We shall never know, but surely the long straight Roman road of Stone Street which runs between Bungay and Halesworth in Suffolk should be a likely place to see a few Roman builders or encounter a skirmish between British tribes and Roman soldiers on a moonlit night? We need to keep our eyes and ears well tuned to the possibility of apparitions, and who knows what may continue to be revealed?

One site in Suffolk that can boast a Roman connection, is the park of Acton House in the village of Acton not far from the village of Little Cornard. The house was built in the eighteenth century, and the garden has one particular spot where there is a tradition that a battle took place during Roman times. Nearby is Wimbell Pond, where an iron chest containing coins is said to be buried. Those who approach the pond and throw a stone, disturbing the calm waters, may hear a plaintive cry echo out 'That's mine... mine... mine!'. Its not recorded, however, whether the chest of coins has a Roman connection. These stories were reported in the eighteenth century, and treasure hidden in ponds and guarded by possessive ghosts are a familiar incident in legends and folklore.

Another site connected with the Romans, between Great and Little Cornard is a field called Shalford Meadow beside the River Stour. It was known as Sharpfight Meadow, and is thought to have been the site of the battle where Boudicca and her tribe of Iceni warriors fought and defeated part of the Roman 9th Legion. She is not known to haunt the spot, but her ghost does hover around the fortress near Epping Upland, in Essex. This is the supposed site where, after her army had suffered inevitable defeat in AD 61, she and her daughters committed suicide by eating poison berries, rather than suffering imprisonment and execution by the hated Roman invaders.

However, Shalford or 'Sharpfight' meadow is also said to have gained its name from a fiery fight between two dragons, recorded in a fifteenth century Chronicle belonging to Canterbury Cathedral.

The ancient boulder that stands near the west door of St Mary's Church in Bungay, is traditionally known as the 'Druid's Stone'. If it is indeed connected with the pagan

5. Roman road with advancing soldiers.

Druidic priesthood it may mark the site of an early Celtic temple. Pagan tribes believed that standing stones were inhabited by gods, who would cause sparks to fly if you tapped upon the stone with a piece of flint or iron pyrites, thus providing the precious gift of fire. The Romans, following their domination of Britain in the first century AD, subdued the native Celtic tribes, and their Druidic religion which involved human sacrifices, was suppressed. They established a strategic fortress at nearby Wainford, just across the River Waveney near Bungay, and so local skirmishes can be imagined before the Bungay temple was finally destroyed. It's another area where the ghosts of Romans or Celts might be imagined to appear, but no encounters are recorded, perhaps because all spectral creatures are frightened out of the churchyard by Bungay's most famous 'spook', the Black Dog.

The 'Druid's Stone' is also known as the 'Devil's Stone'. If you dance around it twelve times, and then tap upon it twelve times, the Devil himself may appear. Alternatively, any question you ask may be answered: for example 'What are this week's winning Lottery numbers?' So far, however, nobody in Bungay has been known to win the Big Lottery prize. The dancing and tapping connection seems as if it may relate back to the Druid temple, because the Stone worship probably involved ritual dancing, and the tapping relates to striking the Stone to produce fire. Wouldn't it be exciting if, on one

6. Druid Stone, St Mary's
Church, Bungay.

dark moonlit night, you tapped upon the Stone, and a Druidic priest appeared? Not so nice, though, if he immediately grabbed you for his next human sacrifice.

With regard to the Danes, who invaded Britain between *c.* 869-917 AD, and fought savage battles with the Saxon inhabitants, the battle sites are deduced from local place names. For example, not far from Bungay at Drayton in Norfolk, it's said that the battle victims were buried in a meadow called 'Bloodsdale'. Another battle is thought to have taken place in Suffolk, near a barrow on Bloodmore Hill, Pakefield, near Lowestoft .

Sites of battles are also indicated by particular plants that flourish where Danish blood was spilt. Dwarf Elder, (*sambucus ebulus),* is still known as Danewort, or Danes Weed, in Suffolk, and is found in various parts of the region.

No Danish hauntings are recorded locally, but it's sometimes said that the spectral hound, Black Shuck, or the Black Dog, is descended from the black hound belonging to the Scandinavian god, Odin. A Black Dog is said to haunt the roads around Earsham, near Bungay, where the Danes sailed up the river and burnt and destroyed village encampments.

Various Suffolk legends are connected with St Edmund, the Saxon king of East Anglia. He was still only a young man when he was killed by the Danes, tied to a tree and shot with arrows at Haegelsidun (thought to be Hoxne in Suffolk) following a battle in 870.

17

7. Roman and Saxon 'Ghosts' return to haunt the ancient town of Bungay.

Within a century of his death he was revered as a martyr, because he died refusing to surrender his Christian faith.

Before his capture, when he was being pursued by his enemies, it's thought that he hid beneath Goldbrook Bridge, on the road between Hoxne and Cross Street. A young couple, just returning from their wedding ceremony, saw the king's gold spurs shining in a reflection from the water and betrayed his hiding place to the Danes. The king therefore laid a curse on any future couples who might pass over the bridge to be married. So his ghostly presence can still affect the lives of young engaged couples today.

Another story is that, following his death, the ghost of St Edmund appeared before the Danish leader Sweyn, and rebuked him for destroying his lands, and struck him with a spear, and on the following day, Sweyn died. St Edmund was buried in the place now associated with his name, Bury St Edmunds, in West Suffolk. The town is much haunted by various ecclesiastical figures, but few people have claimed to have seen St Edmund himself. His most lively memorial is the statue by Elisabeth Frink, in the churchyard near the Cathedral.

2

HAUNTED CASTLES

Following the Norman Conquest in 1066, King William and his French supporters started to build wooden fortresses to defend themselves against the hostile native Saxons. In the following three centuries, local lords and barons constructed more substantial castles of stone, flint and rubble, both as status symbols and as vantage points from which they could wage war against the king, and each other. Many of these ancient castles are associated with ghostly hauntings, but not usually dating from as early as their periods of construction.

One early account, however, relates to Dagworth Castle, in the heart of Suffolk, not far from Stowmarket. It's haunted by a strange spirit called Malekin, described in the Chronicle written by Ralph of Coggeshall in the early thirteenth century. During the reign of Richard I, 1189-1199, Dagworth Castle (which no longer exists) was owned by Osbern of Bradwell. Malekin arrived there one day, and told Osbern's family that she was a changeling who had been stolen as a baby by fairies, while her mother was busy working in the cornfield nearby. She had lived with the fairies for seven years, and they had told her that when she was seven years older, she would be allowed to return to the human world again. Although she was invisible to the family, she appeared in a physical form to a servant who had particularly befriended her, and who described her as a little girl wearing a white dress.

Having stayed with the family for a short period, she disappeared and was never seen again. Unless of course, the fairies kept their promise and after seven years she was freed to live a normal life in human form. But it seems more likely that she was scolded for having dared to converse with humans, and punished by never being permitted to return to the mortal world again. If so, her tearful troubled spirit may still haunt the site of mediaeval Dagworth Castle, searching for the family and the servant girl who had been so kind to her. Of all the ghosts connected with Suffolk, she would be one of the most delightful to encounter.

Framlingham Castle and Bungay Castle were both built in the twelfth century by members of the Bigod clan, a Norman family who had come to England with William the Conqueror in 1066. Bungay Castle was Hugh Bigod's chief residence, which he had built in c. 1165 with the boast that it was one of the most impregnable fortresses in the kingdom. He was regularly in combat with the reigning monarchs, and eventually incurred the wrath of Henry II, with the result that the king marched a huge army down to Suffolk, forced Hugh to submit, and organised the destruction of his properties in the area. Both castles were partly demolished: Hugh paid a huge fine of a thousand silver marks to preserve Bungay Castle from complete destruction, but Framlingham Castle was substantially knocked down by Alnodus the royal engineer.

Both castles were reoccupied by later generations of the Bigod family. Framlingham was rebuilt on a larger scale in the 1180's by Roger Bigod, and Bungay was modernised and provided with a protective curtain wall and gatehouse by another Roger Bigod in 1294. In the fifteenth century these and other Bigod estates passed to the Howard family, Dukes of Norfolk. Framlingham became their main residence, and Bungay Castle, largely uninhabited, was left to fall into decay.

Bungay Castle is haunted by both Hugh Bigod, who died in *c.* 1176, and later generations of the Bigod family. Known as the 'Bold, Bad Bigods', they were such a wild crew that it's easy to understand why their turbulent spirits could never rest in peace. One local historian, Morley Adams, records that they were so notorious for cruelty and crimes, that their punishment was to haunt forever the spots where their wicked deeds had been perpetrated.

Hugh Bigod is believed to haunt the Bungay area in the guise of the Black Dog (see Chapter 4). Younger members of the family can be observed travelling on certain nights of the year in a coach, drawn by horses with flames and smoke pouring from their nostrils. The coach is driven by a headless coachman, his head tucked under his arm. No more terrifying sight can be imagined in the narrow roads and lanes around Bungay on a dark moonless night. The coach is said to travel from the town along the top road to Geldeston, near Beccles, past Geldeston church, along the path called Lovers Lane, then down a narrow sandy track known as Bigods' Hill, onto the 'low' road, and so back to Bungay. It is said never to be both *seen* and *heard*. Witnesses either hear it approaching with rattling wheels, snorting horses, and pounding hooves, but see nothing, or else they observe a phantom coach which glides silently by and then disappears from view along one or other of the roads described.

In the eighteenth century the Georgian writer Elizabeth Bonhote (1744-1818), bought the ruined Bungay Castle from the Duke of Norfolk. She was so fascinated by its romantic history, that she published a novel about it, in two volumes, *Bungay Castle*, 1796. It proved a great popular success with readers of the period, and has recently been republished. In the introduction, she describes how, during her youth in Bungay she heard tales related about the Castle by:

'the old and superstitious'. In one place, it was said the ghost of an ancient warrior clad in armour, took his nightly round to reconnoitre scenes endeared by many a tender claim. In another, a lovely female form had been seen to glide along, and was supposed to disappear on the very spot where it was imagined her lover had fallen a victim to the contention of the times:
'Her face was like an April sky,
Dimm'd by a scatt'ring cloud;
Her clay-cold lily hand, knee-high
Held up her sable shroud'.

Both these hauntings seem to relate to the mediaeval period, when the Castle was occupied by the Bigods, as the 'contention of the times' refers to the Barons' wars of the twelfth and thirteenth centuries. The ghost of a young woman, clad in white has been

Above: 8. Bungay Castle in the
eighteenth century.

Right: 9. Phantom horses.

seen in the vicinity of the castle grounds in recent years, and verified by two witnesses. It's not clear whether she relates to the young woman mentioned by Eliza Bonhote, as no 'sable shroud' is mentioned, so she may be a more recent phantom figure.

There have always been rumours in the town about underground tunnels and dungeons connecting the town centre and Castle, and, in her novel, Elizabeth even describes a tunnel stretching to the Benedictine Priory and to another castle about three miles distant. These may have been imagined solely to make the novel of greater interest, so cannot be taken too seriously. However, the stories of town centre passages and dungeons seemed to obtain some justification, when the following report was published in the *Norfolk News*, March, 1883:

> During the progress of some excavations in the yard of the King's Head Hotel, on the site of the old Norman Castle, the workmen came upon a slab of stone. This with great difficulty being removed, disclosed a spiral stone staircase. After a sufficient time to allow the escape of bad air, a descent was made by Mr Candler, Jnr., and Mr James Hawes, a tradesman of this town.
>
> At the foot of the staircase was a vault, 48 ft long, by 30 ft wide, supported on two rows of Norman columns. Judging by the remains of chains and fragments of bones at one end of the vault, it is presumed that it was used as the dungeon of the castle in which it is recorded that Sir Hugh Biggott [sic], practised great cruelties in the reign of King Stephen.
>
> The remainder of the vault contained portions of armour, five battleaxes in wonderful preservation, and a crock of silver coins, the value of which it is as yet impossible to judge, their weight alone being over 13 pounds. In the early traditions of this town, such a chamber or vault has often been mentioned, though I think no one has ever attached much credence to it.

Unfortunately, it seems that this story was just a spoof dreamed up by an enterprising young journalist, but the stories of secret underground passages and dungeons continue to be circulated in the town. During excavations around the central keep in 1933, a large dungeon area was found, but it had been filled with earth and rubble for centuries, and nothing more interesting was found than a few scattered bits of pottery, and a wooden seat for the garderobe, the mediaeval term for a lavatory, still intact in the adjacent chamber. However, much of the area is still unexcavated, and, who knows, one day a grim discovery of skeletons chained to the walls of a vault, may still be discovered in this ancient town with its wealth of historic and spooky associations.

The other remaining Bigod castle at Framlingham, (a third, Walton, was destroyed in the twelfth century) is the best preserved castle in Suffolk. Bad vibes connected with the family must certainly foul the air around it, but strangely, no particular ghost stories concerning the Bigod's occupation seem to be circulated.

After the demise of the Bigod family, Framlingham became the main residence of the Howard family from 1480. They rebuilt and refurbished parts of it in the Tudor period, adding the ornate chimneys which were considered fashionable at the time, but to modern eyes appear incongruous in connection with the mediaeval fabric.

When Thomas Howard, 3rd Duke, fell out of favour with Henry VIII in 1546, the king confiscated Framlingham, and the castle was inherited by his daughter Mary Tudor.

It was while she was living at Framlingham that she received the news of her brother, Edward VI's, death, and her accession to the throne, and she issued her first royal commands from the Castle on 20 July 1553. Shortly afterwards she pardoned Thomas Howard and so he was released from the Tower, and enabled to take possession of the Castle again.

It's Queen Mary who is associated with hauntings there. She became unpopular throughout the country, but particularly in parts of Suffolk due to her policy of having those who would not accept the Catholic faith burnt at the stake. Thirty-six people were executed in Suffolk alone. One of them was Rowland Taylor, Rector of Hadleigh, near Ipswich. He was charged with heresy and condemned to the cruel death by burning in 1555. From Mary's point of view, he would be condemned by God to eternal hell-fire anyhow, so it didn't matter if he suffered a brief spell of burning during his mortal life.

She became nicknamed 'Bloody Mary', and when it was rumoured that she had given birth to a child at Framlingham, gossip related that it was not a child but a viper or serpent, while others insisted it was a Devil. The malicious assertion is reported in an eighteenth century volume, M. de Lazowski's *Lettres a un Ami*, first published in 1784, and reprinted by Suffolk Records Society, Vol. XXX, in 1988. With this demonic local reputation, it's not surprising if she is thought to haunt the castle and its precincts. Bob Roberts, the present Chair of Trustees of the Lanman Museum at the Castle reports that

10. Framlingham Castle.

11. 'Doom' detail from the fifteenth century panel painting in Wenhaston Church.

the small chamber in which Mary is said to have given birth is part of the Museum area. However, he's not aware that any haunting activity has occurred within the chamber during his period of association with the building. Mary is also rumoured to appear at Sawston Hall in Cambridgeshire, a house she had built in 1553, where her ghost lingers in the room in which she slept, and invisible hands fiddle with the door-latch.

Mary, of course, never succeeded in having a child, and after her short and unhappy reign, her sister Elizabeth I became queen in 1558. The Howard family ceased to occupy Framlingham Castle, and it became a prison for Recusants during the remainder of Elizabeth's reign. Recusants were Catholics who refused to accept the Protestant changes in religion, so it's rather ironic – or perhaps entirely appropriate – that they should be imprisoned in Mary Tudor's former residence. It's unlikely that her ghost would linger around to frighten the lives out of those of her own religious faith, so perhaps that's why she's better known in a spirit guise at Sawston Hall.

Demons of the type which Mary was said to have spawned, were the subject of much superstition throughout the mediaeval and Tudor periods. The Protestant clergy tried to eradicate these primitive beliefs but without great success. A wonderful panel painting of demons pushing and prodding sinners into the jaws of Hell, known as the 'Doom' can be seen in Wenhaston Church, near Halesworth. Thought to have been commissioned from by a monk at Blythburgh Priory, it was painted in *c.* 1480. It's a rare complete survival of a 'Last Judgement' style of composition, and vividly illustrates how Christians of the period visualised life after death, and what they could expect, depending on whether they had lived virtuous or sinful lives. Demons, tempting them to sin, or taunting or haunting them were more of a terrifying reality than the ghosts of dead humans returning from the grave.

Just as Moyse's Hall Museum provides an ideal starting point for a Ghost Tour of Suffolk, so a visit to the Wenhaston 'Doom' will provide an intriguing insight into the 'haunted' imaginations of ordinary people before the advancement of science, and a greater understanding of the natural world, developed in the seventeenth and eighteenth centuries.

3

MONASTIC MURMURINGS

When Henry VIII decided to close all the monasteries and priories during the Reformation period, 1536-40, they were sold for government expenditure, and purchased by wealthy families throughout the kingdom. The monks and nuns resident in these buildings were obliged to disperse. The men were usually able to find new roles within the church, or as clerks or teachers, but the situation for women was rather different. There was little employment open to women of the middle and upper-classes in the sixteenth century and although most of the nuns received pensions, they were usually obliged to return home to live with their families or whoever else was prepared to provide them with accommodation. In Bungay, when the Benedictine Priory closed in 1536, it seems that all the nuns dispersed apart from the Prioress, Lady Elizabeth Sherborne. She continues to be mentioned in the Churchwardens' accounts, and as the priest at St Mary's in 1545 is also named Sherborne, he is likely to have been related to her and perhaps explains the reason why she remained in the town.

The haunting of nuns and monks in the vicinity of ecclesiastical buildings is common, and some of these restless souls probably began haunting their monastic homes, after the Dissolution: those places where they had been secure and happy before they were obliged to depart. Some, however, may have been insecure and unhappy. One particular young novice at the Bungay Priory had been not just unhappy but positively wretched. Imagine the situation. You are a teenage girl, attractive, high-spirited, a member of a wealthy and aristocratic family. You are looking forward to a buzzing social life, being courted by handsome and wealthy young men from the best families in Suffolk; then a distinguished marriage to a local Lord, and becoming mistress of a large landed estate. Then suddenly one day your father calls you into his private chamber. He tells you that for his own good reasons, which you must not question, you are to be entered as a novice at The Benedictine Priory of the Holy Cross, thirty miles distant from your home. There, cut off from the rest of the world, you will be trained for Holy Orders, and at the culmination of your novitiate you will take the binding vows to make you a Bride of Christ. You will then remain immured in the Nunnery for the remainder of your life. You may never see your family again, your life will be one of prayer, charity, and deprivation, and you will never have the opportunity to marry or bear children. You might just as well have been told that you are to be banished to a prison-cell, or a sepulchral earthly tomb.

This was the sad fate that befell young Katherine de Montacute, in about the year 1375. She came from one of the most prominent families in the region. The coat of arms of the Montacute family are displayed on the tower of Bungay Holy Trinity church, and Sir Edward de Montacute had inherited Bungay Castle and several manors from his marriage in *c.* 1360. His daughter married William de Ufford, Earl of Suffolk. Another Montacute had been one of the chief benefactors of the Bungay Priory which is probably one reason why Katherine, perhaps the grand-daughter or niece, of Sir Edward, was enrolled there.

Unhappy Katherine. How she must have inwardly rebelled against such a cruel and unjust fate. But in those days, children were obliged to obey their parents. It was written in the Ten Commandments, and disobedience was a terrible sin. Katherine struggled to comply with both her parents' wishes, and the strict regime of the monastic life. Yet, after a while she could bear it no longer. Early one morning, while the rest of the nuns were engaged in silent devotion in their cells, she managed to steal out of the dismal, cold, damp Priory building, and escape! It seems she must have had an accomplice, who was able to provide some money, and a means of getting out of the building, the grounds of which were surrounded by high flint-faced walls. He must also have provided her with a change of clothing, because when her disappearance was detected it was reported that she was wearing not the dark robes and veil of a Benedictine novitiate, but the fashionable costume of an aristocratic lady. Perhaps her helper was a brother, or maybe even a sweetheart, to whom she had become secretly betrothed before her father ended all her dreams of getting married and living happily ever after.

12. St Mary's Church and Priory, Bungay.

A document housed in the Tower of London reports an order for the arrest of the fugitive, described as:

> wandering and fleeing from parish to parish, in divers parts of England, in secular dress, in peril of her soul, and to the manifest scandal of the order of St Benedict.

A scandal indeed! We don't know exactly what happened, or how long Katherine managed to evade her pursuers, or whether she was alone, or accompanied by her accomplice or sweetheart. Yet she could not have enjoyed freedom for very long. Four years later, her name is recorded as the Prioress of the Bungay convent! How could such a radical change of attitude have occurred? In order to attain that high office within a comparatively short time, she must have been soon detected, and obliged to return, and then lived a life of meticulous adherence to the daily routine and devotions of the Benedictine order.

Perhaps she realised that a life of freedom, and the possibility of marriage were not to be, and resigned herself to her fate. It's difficult to know whether to feel sorry or pleased for her, but life as the Prioress carried a great deal of prestige, and many perks, including social entertaining, some degree of fashionable apparel, and the best of foods at certain times of the year when fasting was not required. And if she enjoyed embroidery, she had ample time to indulge the hobby. 'Bungay work' from the Priory became celebrated in the mediaeval period for its fine detail, and a number of churches and monasteries acquired examples for either display or worn as clerical vestments. It is recorded that her hatchment – painted or embroidered armorial bearings – remained in the Priory church for many years after her death which occurred in 1396.

So perhaps we don't have to feel too sorry for Katherine. Certainly, if her ghost still haunts the churchyard of St Mary's it's a cheerful one. She will be glimpsed, not in the dead of night but in the first dim rays of dawn, strolling among the Priory ruins, wearing a gilt embroidered gown, and humming a cheerful tune. But this relates, not to her monastic career, but to the exciting morning of her bid for escape and freedom!

Bury St Edmunds, particularly the region of the Abbey Gate and Abbey gardens, is also haunted by monastic figures, monks, not nuns, and none with such an interesting story as Katherine's. The town has been identified as one of the most spiritually powerful places in England, and stands on the St Michael's Line, the leyline which links many significant ancient sites. Ghosts of monks have also been seen in various buildings in Abbeygate street leading towards the town centre.

Following the Dissolution of the monasteries, and the selling of church buildings and lands, there was a widespread belief that acquiring church property in this way would bring a curse upon the new owners.

It certainly seems to have been the case with Thomas Howard, 3rd Duke of Norfolk, who obtained Bungay Priory by about 1539. His niece, Catherine Howard, who married Henry VIII as his fifth wife, was executed for adultery. His son, Henry Howard, Earl of Surrey, was executed for treason in 1547, and Thomas, believed to be implicated in the plot, was imprisoned by Henry VIII in the Tower of London, and only escaped execution himself because Henry died before he could sign the death warrant. The 4th duke was also executed for treason in 1572, so the Howard family got their fair share of retribution. Later, the Black Dog haunted the Bungay Priory church site, and

13. Barsham Church.

his presence may also have been connected with the doomed Howard family and the 'Reformation Property' curse.

A similar curse is connected with the Blennerhassett family, and Barsham, a small village near Beccles. Monk's Grange, at St James's Hill, Thorpe, on the outskirts of Norwich, was an ecclesiastical property occupied by the Prior of Norwich in the mediaeval period. Following the Dissolution it was leased to William Blennerhassett, and the property soon gained the reputation of being haunted. Strange sights and sounds were experienced there, some terrified witnesses had seen a dead body roll across the floor in one particular room, and some of the doors couldn't be opened no matter how hard you tugged at them. Two doors were discovered that had been plastered over, and when the workmen attempted to uncover them, they became blinded.

The Blennerhassett family also acquired property at Barsham, and it's in that vicinity that a ghastly and ghostly haunting takes place. A member of the family, recognised only as 'Old Blunderhazard', drives out in a coach from his Barsham house each year on Christmas Eve at midnight. The coach travels to Hassett's Tower, returning to Barsham on the following morning. The horses pulling the coach are headless, and yet some observers have reported that they had fire and smoke streaming from their nostrils. Nineteenth century traditions in Norwich record that when the coach reaches the city, it takes the route over Bishop's Bridge, and then onto Mousehold Heath. The crack of the coach-driver's whip is heard, and sparks fly from the coach, which is sometimes seen flying up above the houses and shops. In the Norwich accounts, the occupant of the coach is called simply 'old Hasset', and he is said to be returning to his haunted property of Monk's Grange, or Hassett's Manor, as it was later known. The house was demolished in 1792, and became the site of the cavalry barracks. In the *East Anglian Handbook* for 1885, John Varden reports that by that date the property was well-known for being haunted.

It has to be pointed out that there are at least three different stories connected with phantom coaches on the Beccles to Bungay roads, and one wonders whether they are variant accounts of the same event. A horse drawn coach with a headless groom travels out from Roos Hall on Christmas Eve, and this house on the outskirts of Beccles, is at the top of the road leading to Barsham. The Bigod's coach also travels to Geldeston which is in the vicinity of Barsham and Roos Hall. Why should there be such a plethora of phantom coaches and headless horses in this small area of the Waveney Valley? And could it result in a deathly collision on the highway one dark night?

Throughout the Reformation, terrible incidents involving evil spirits, blood-chilling hauntings, and all manner of catastrophes were felt to be inevitable. This was particularly the case following the reigns of Henry VIII and Edward VI. These monarchs were criticised by many for having robbed the churches of all the sacred religious objects that had provided a protective magic for parishioners throughout the previous centuries. Henry VIII had instigated the changes by severing connections with the Catholic papacy in Rome to establish the Church of England, and curbing the cult of images of saints in churches, and the destruction of holy shrines. His son, Edward VI, went further in establishing Protestantism as a form of religion governed strictly by the word of God as revealed in the Bible, and banning all superstitious imagery and objects. So every church throughout the land, which in the mediaeval period had been colourfully and richly decorated with wall paintings, statues, carved images, and a wide variety of religious relics, was stripped bare, stained glass removed from the windows, the wall paintings white-washed over, paintings, embroideries, statues and carvings, destroyed or sold.

The church interiors were unrecognisable compared with how they had been in previous times. The majority of the population, who had no particular interest in Protestant theology, were shocked and bewildered. They had tended to believe that all the imagery and objects, painted, embroidered or carved, connected with the Holy Family and saints, had magical powers which could protect them, their families, and even their homes and farm animals, from harm. Now that these were removed, surely they were exposed to all manner of attacks by Satan and his malicious army of demons, sprites, and bogie beasts?

It was in this context that the Black Dog event in the churches of Bungay and Blythburgh must be understood. This phantom hound, understood to be 'The Devil in such a likenesse', was only able to gain entry to the church, and cause deaths, injuries and destruction, because the holy objects that had previously rendered it secure had been removed and destroyed. So there was no longer any safe place left to shield yourself from Satan and his mischief making. The Black Dog events will be dealt with in detail in the following chapter.

Nor could the church provide protection against witchcraft. Witches were men or women who used their powers of magic to cast harmful spells on humans, animals, or property, although there were also the 'White Witches' who could use similar powers for human good. Witchcraft was only made illegal in 1542, during the reign of Henry VIII, after his severance from the Church of Rome, and was at least partly the consequence of the religious disorientation caused by the Reformation. Thereafter witches could

14. Anne Boleyn.

be hanged if their use of 'magic' could be deemed to have resulted in deaths, or they could be imprisoned, fined, or put in the pillory or stocks, for less serious offences. A number of trials and executions of witches took place in Suffolk in the late sixteenth and seventeenth centuries. Witches were reported to conjure up ghosts and visions for their own purposes, but although there are many accounts of witches and their activities in Suffolk, none are particularly related to ghostly apparitions.

It's ironic that Anne Boleyn, Henry VIII's second wife, and the chief reason for his break with Rome, because the Pope would not permit the king's divorce from Catherine of Aragon, was believed by many to be a witch. She had red hair, which was a bad sign, and a strong character, which was worse. When Henry became bored with her, and frustrated with her failure to produce a son, she was beheaded on trumped-up charges of adultery in 1536. There was widespread public disgust, and particularly in Suffolk, where Anne had spent much of her childhood living with her aunt at Erwarton near Shotley Gate on the Stour estuary. The aunt, Amata Boleyn, married a man called Calthorpe, and their home was Erwarton Hall. During Anne's residence there, it's said that Henry VIII commenced his courtship of her, visiting her in his royal yacht. It was an exciting and romantic period for the young girl, and she and Henry were eventually married in 1533.

Romance soon turned into disillusion, and, after only three years of marriage, Anne's failure to produce a male heir signalled the end of Henry's infatuation with her. It's likely that, after her execution in the Tower of London, where many of Henry's former friends and lovers ended up, her body together with her severed head was buried in the Tower chapel. But there's a tradition, no doubt emanating from Suffolk, that her heart was actually brought to Erwarton and buried in the local church.

The journal *Norfolk Archaeology*, in 1884, recorded the discovery in 1837 of a lead, heart-shaped casket, which was presumed in the parish to contain the heart of the tragic queen. It was reburied in the Cornwallis vault beneath the organ. There is no supporting evidence to verify the claim. Heart burials occur from time to time, but in the absence of any other claimant to this particular heart, it's easy to understand why local people wished to believe that after a tragic marriage and death, the heart of the young queen was brought home to the village where she had spent her happy and innocent youth. The authors of *The Lore of the Land*, conclude in their accounts of the Erwarton connection: 'Anne Boleyn has become a figure of romance, her ghost haunting more places than any other historical person'. She is certainly the most celebrated ghost connected with Suffolk.

To some extent she was the victim of her father's desire for his daughter to achieve royal status. For her own part, she must have found the king's domineering and persuasive personality difficult to resist, and whether she was 'in love' with him or not, she would be tempted to accept the role of the most important and glamorous woman in the kingdom, with riches and luxury untold. Also, she was only his second choice of wife: she was not to know the extent of Henry's cruelty and selfishness and that four other wives would follow after her, of whom another, Catherine Howard, was destined for the scaffold. And in Catherine's case, with better reason, since it seems clear that she had committed adultery whereas with Anne it was just a trumped-up excuse to get rid of her.

It's terrible to think that the romance which had commenced with such promise at Erwarton, ended in great personal tragedy. Anne suffered unhappiness and humiliating

15. The White Lady, Covehithe churchyard.

guilt from the knowledge that she could not produce Henry's longed for male heir. She had the indignity of being falsely accused of sexual liaisons. And she had the heartbreaking awareness that a number of young men were to be tortured and beheaded on the pretext that they had been her lovers: with the expectation that her own beheading would soon follow. A crueller fate cannot be imagined. It's hardly surprising if, after her death, her troubled ghost returned to linger at Erwarton, to wander about the gardens and seek again those happy and carefree days before her courtship with Henry had turned into a doomed betrothal. Truly, her heart belongs at Erwarton.

Both Anne and her father, Sir Thomas Boleyn, haunt Blickling Hall the family home in Norfolk. Like the traditions of Suffolk coaches, a phantom vehicle drives up to the door of the Hall. It's drawn by headless horses, and inside sits Anne, holding her severed head in her hand. At the door of the house, Anne enters, and glides through the rooms, although perhaps less often now that the property is regularly thronged with National Trust visitors. Sir Thomas, who is by some held responsible for Anne's betrothal to the king, is also a doomed figure, compelled to ride once a year over forty bridges in Norfolk and Suffolk. Hopefully, not in the Bungay and Beccles region, or there would be even more phantom coach congestion after dark!

Another Tudor haunting in Suffolk is connected with Seckford Hall near Woodbridge. Thomas Seckford was the Master of the Court of Requests during the reign of Elizabeth I. His town house was Woodbridge Abbey, and it may be that, like Thomas Howard, Duke of Norfolk, he was cursed with bad luck as a consequence of acquiring church property following the Dissolution.

There's a tradition that a secret passage connected Woodbridge Abbey with Seckford Hall, a red brick mansion with an elegant Tudor façade, built in *c.* 1530 by Seckford's father. Seckford donated money to a number of charities in the Woodbridge area. He died in 1585, and his tomb and monument, which also commemorates his two wives and two sons, can still be seen in the north chapel of St Mary's church in Woodbridge.

Seckford Hall fell into decay in subsequent centuries, but more recently has been restored, and opened as a hotel and restaurant. It's said that Thomas Seckford haunts the building, dressed in elaborate Tudor costume, with a high-crowned hat, and carrying his staff of office. He mutters and complains that the money he endowed for the Seckford Trust to benefit poor families in the town, was mis-handled by his executors and used for other purposes.

Churchyard hauntings are widespread in Suffolk, with its large number of churches, and because spirits often linger in the places where their mortal remains are buried. Covehithe is on the Suffolk coast between the popular seaside towns of Lowestoft and Southwold. Although much smaller and without the same attractions and amenities, it remains very popular with visitors who prefer a quieter and less commercial resort. The churchyard is said to be haunted by the White Lady. When seen there at night she appears all shrouded in white, but as her ghostly figure draws closer she suddenly draws aside her hood and you realise with horror, that she has no face! Her name and history are unknown. The church of St Andrew's is of medieval origin, but had fallen into ruin by the seventeenth century and a smaller church was built within the walls of the old one. Perhaps the White Lady's tomb was disturbed or destroyed during the re-building, and that's why she haunts the spot today.

4

THE BLACK DOG OF BUNGAY

More than four hundred years ago, the clerk of St Mary's church, Bungay, wrote in the Churchwarden's Register: '1577, 4th of August, being Sunday, such Thunder, lightning, rayne and darkenesse, as never was sene ye lyke. Never to be Forgotten'.

And to this day, it never has been. It was not only the most fearful storm ever to have struck Bungay, but while it raged, the congregation of the church fell to their knees screaming in panic. For the Black Dog had suddenly appeared amongst them. That fateful event is now the best known story connected with the town, and has captured the imagination of people all over the world, resulting in books, television documentaries, dramatic re-enactments, and hundreds of visitors coming to the town each year to find out where it all happened.

An account of what occured was recorded, very soon after the event, by the Reverend Abraham Fleming. Fleming was the Rector of St Pancras Church in London, and published his report in a pamphlet entitled: *A Straunge and Terrible Wunder wrought very late in the Parish Church of Bungay*. He was not a local man, and may never have visited Bungay, but he affirms that his story is based on the accounts of eye-witnesses, those who had been in the church during the storm. He was a Puritan clergyman of the 'Hell & Damnation' type, and his reason for publishing the pamphlet was to draw to people's attention his belief that Bungay people had been subjected to a terrible ordeal as punishment for bad behaviour It was God's timely warning to them to improve their ways and repent of their sins, or worse terrors might follow. If they, and all other sinners, refuse to live Christian lives, Satan, the Prince of Darkness, will be empowered to spread his influence over the nation, resulting in an extreme 'Sodomitical or Babylonical destruction'.

The pamphlet commences by setting the scene of the event:

Sunday, being the fourth of this August, in ye year of our Lord, 1577, to the amazing and singular astonishment of the present beholders, and absent hearers, at a certain town called Bungay, not past ten miles distant from the city of Norwich, there fell from heaven an exceeding great and terrible tempest, sudden and violent, between nine of the clock in the morning and ten of the day aforesaid.

The parishioners of St Mary's church had assembled to attend the customary Sunday morning service. It was shortly after worship had commenced that the tempest occurred, and they became the:

16. The Black Dog of Bungay.

17. The Black Dog in St Mary's Church.

witnesses of the strangeness, the rareness, and suddenness of the storm, consisting of rain violently falling, fearful flashes of lightning, and terrible cracks of thunder, which came with such unwonted force and power, that to the perceiving of the people,... the church did as it were quake and stagger, which struck into the hearts of those that were present, such a sore and sudden fear, that they were in a manner robbed of their right wits.

In this frightening situation, and praying to God for mercy, they suddenly saw, in the midst of the church, a black dog, which, illuminated in the bright flashes of lightning fire, caused such apprehension that 'they thought Doomsday had already come'.

The dog, described as being 'the Devil in such a likeness', ran down the main aisle between the rows of parishioners who by this time, were all on their knees still pleading for help, or shielding their eyes from the lightning and the horrible apparition. He suddenly lunged at two of them, and, as Fleming dramatically describes it:

wrung the necks of them both at one instant clean backwards, insomuch that, even at that moment where they kneeled, they strangely died.

The dog:

still continuing and remaining in one and the self same shape, passing by another man of the congregation... gave him such a grip on the back, that therewith all he was

18. St Mary's Church, Bungay.

presently drawn together and shrunk up, as it were a piece of leather scorched in a hot fire; or as the mouth of a purse or bag, drawn together with a string. The man, albeit he was in so strange a taking, died not, but as it is thought is yet alive: which thing is marvellous in the eyes of men, and offereth much matter of amazing the mind.

This is a most vivid description of the deaths and injuries sustained, and tends to confirm that Fleming was indeed basing his narrative on eye-witness accounts. He goes on to describe what was happening outside the church. The clerk had gone to clean the gutter when the storm started, and during another clap of thunder and flash of lightning was violently thrown to the ground. Miraculously, he suffered no injuries, providing Fleming with another opportunity to thank God for his tender mercies: 'Oh Lord, how wonderful art thou in thy works!'

Apart from the eye-witness reports, Fleming then states that the evidence for his startling story remains for all to see:

As testimony and witnesses of the force which rested in this strange shaped thing [the Dog], there are remaining in the stones of the church and likewise in the church door which are marvellously rent and torn, the marks as it were of his claws or talons. Beside, that all the wires, the wheels, and other things belonging to the clock [in the church tower], were wrung asunder and broken in pieces.

19. Blythburgh Church.

The dog he says, then vanished from the church, and shortly afterwards appeared in St Mary's at Blythburgh, about ten miles distant from Bungay. He entered

'in the same shape and similitude, where, placing himself upon a main balk or beam, whereon the Rood [a large carving of Christ on the Cross] did stand, suddenly he gave a swing down into the church, and there also, as before, slew two men, and a lad, and burned the hand of another person, that was there among the rest of the company, of whom divers were blasted'.

'This mischief thus wrought, he flew, with wonderful force to no little fear of the assembly, out of the church in a hideous and hellish likeness'.

Fleming concludes by asserting that his account is true, as reported by eye-witnesses of both events, and then adds an admonishing sermon:

Let us pray unto God, as it is the duty of Christians, to work all things to the best, to turn our flinty hearts into fleshly hearts, that we may feel the fire of God's mercy, and flee from the scourge of his justice.

This is the account, circulated in a pamphlet in London, Suffolk, and probably other parts of the country, upon which the famous legend of the Black Dog of Bungay is based. However, there were some other records of the occurrence made at the time, or shortly afterwards.

Raphael Holinshed, a London printer, was the producer of a compendium of information about the history of Britain, up to his own times, entitled *The Chronicles of England, Scotland and Ireland*. It was written by a number of different collaborators, and published in 1578. An extended edition followed in 1586, for which Abraham Fleming was one of the contributors. Like Fleming's pamphlet about the Black Dog event, Holinshed's writings frequently interpret catastrophes as God's judgement upon the sinful ways of mankind. In particular extreme weather conditions such as thunderstorms could be interpreted: 'as tokens of God's wrath ready bent against the world for sin now abounding... who doeth only thus but to shew us the rod wherewith we daily deserve to be beaten'.

He includes an account of a storm at Blasedon in Yorkshire:

After a great tempest of lightning and thunder, a woman of four score years old [i.e. eighty], named Alice Perrin, was delivered of an hideous monster, whose head was like unto a sallet or headpiece, the face like unto a man's except the mouth which was round and small like unto the mouth of a mouse, the forepart of the body like to a man, having eight legs not one like another and a tail half a yard long... [God sends] many such significant warnings before he taketh the rod in hand and whippeth us till we smart.

Holinshed and his fellow Protestant writers therefore link unusual events with thunderstorms, and even an old woman being unfortunate enough to give birth to a deformed child is seen as a sign of God's wrath.

The Chronicle also includes an account of the terrible storm in Bungay:

On Sunday, the fourth of August between the hours of nine and ten of the clock in the forenoon, whilst the minister was reading of the second lesson in the parish church of Bliborough [Blythburgh] a town in Suffolk, a strange and terrible tempest of lightning and thunder struck through the wall of the same church into the ground a yard deep, drew down all the people on that side, above twenty persons, then renting the wall up to the vestry, cleft the door, and returning to the steeple, rent the timber, broke the chimes, and fled towards Bungay a town six [actually ten] miles off.

The people that were stricken down were found grovelling more than half an hour after, whereof one man more than forty years, and a boy of fifteen years old were found stark dead; the others were scorched. The same or the like flash of lightning and cracks of thunder rent the parish church of Bungay, nine miles [actually fifteen] from Norwich, wrung in sunder the wires and wheels of the clocks, slew two men which sat in the belfry, when the others were at the procession of suffrages, and scorched another, which hardly escaped.

Although written at roughly the same time as Fleming's pamphlet, this account contains many differences. In addition, it has no moralising or 'supernatural' elements, and is similar to how a journalist might record a catastrophe in our newspapers today.

The writer makes Blythburgh, rather than Bungay, the main feature of his account. He also states that at Bungay it was two men sitting in the belfry who were killed, not amongst the congregation in the church. And, most significantly of all, there is no mention of a Satanic Black Dog. The deaths of the people involved, and the damage to the churches, is described as due entirely to severe strikes of lightning during the thunderstorm.

Holinshed's account is similar to the entries made in the St Mary's Churchwardens' Register of Accounts for that year: 'Item paid to the four poor women that laid forth the bodies of the two men that were stricken dead both within the steeple of the church at the great tempest that was on the 4th of August, 1577'.

In the margin, somebody has added: 'A great, terrible and fearful tempest at the time of Procession upon the Sunday. Such darkness, rain, hail, thunder & lightning as was never seen the like'.

The Parish Burial Register provides the names of the two men who were killed: 'John Fuller and Adam Walker, slain in the Tempest in the Belfry in the time of prayer upon the Lord's Day the 4th of August, 1577'.

In the margin, somebody has added: *'THE TEMPEST OF THUNDER'*.

Two years later, in 1579, another reference appeared in the Churchwardens' Accounts Register:

Item: 'Paid to a carpenter for seven days work with meat and wages for mending and repairing the chyngling [glazing bars] of the steeple window at the east side, that was broken and jagged in pieces at the great tempest of thunder and lightning that was at Bungay the 4th of August being Sunday in AD 1577, when two of the parishioners were stricken dead in the Bellhouse, and died, some others of the parishioners stricken down to the ground and some hurt in diverse places of their legs and feet, to the great fears of all the parishioners'.

20. Door of Blythburgh church with the scorched claw-marks of the Black Dog.

In the margin, somebody has added: '1577, 4th August, being Sunday, such thunder, lightning, rain and darkness as never was seen the like. Never to be forgotten'.

All these accounts present the same story, and no mention is made of a Black Dog. The deaths, injuries, and damage to the church building are all ascribed to lightning strikes, and the fact that two Suffolk churches not far from each other were affected, testifies to the unusual ferocity of the storm.

Yet it cannot be assumed that just because the 'official' records make no mention of a savage, spectral beast, that no such creature was involved. Clearly some of the parishioners thought that 'the devil in such a likeness' was amongst them and was responsible for the disaster, whereas the Holinshed chroniclers, and the parish clerks might have good reason for not wishing to include any reference to the beast in their records. All testify to the extraordinary ferocity of the occurrence, but the cause of it was a matter of personal belief and speculation.

In the previous chapter, the point is made that, following the changes to the interior of churches during the Reformation, many believed that the buildings had been robbed of the protective religious magic that had served the community for generations. In Bungay, the changes that had occurred followed the same pattern as throughout the rest of the country. In the reign of Henry VIII, there was a ban on images relating to Saint Thomas Becket, and stained glass, embroideries, and other memorials relating to him in the Bungay churches were destroyed, causing distress to those who had a particular veneration for the saint. When Henry's son, Edward VI became king in 1547, it was decreed that all images and superstitious objects must be removed from the churches, and the St Mary's churchwardens' accounts record: 'Item: received (payment) for certain tabernacles and images which were taken out of the church'.

Tabernacles were the canopied niches or recesses in the wall designed to contain images of the Holy Family and saints. Further payments are made to a man called Patten, for erasing the painted depictions of saints and religious stories on the church walls, and to John Packe for erasing, or removing stained glass in the windows, and white-washing over the large depiction of St Christopher facing the entrance porch. St Christopher was greatly venerated in the mediaeval period. He was the patron saint of travellers, protecting them on their journeys, and it was also believed that if you looked at his image as soon as you entered the building, you could be protected from suffering death before your absolution for sins had been dealt with by a priest. This was an important consideration in the mediaeval period, when death without forgiveness of sins could result in a swift descent into Hell fire: the sort of fate so vividly depicted in the Wenhaston 'Doom' painting.

Other objects in the church were believed to have special powers to protect the parishioners. Some of the congregation would even conceal the communion wafers during Mass and carry them away to use as talismans against misfortune. In Canterbury, in 1543, when a thunderstorm occurred, the local people ran into the church to collect holy water from the font to sprinkle on their houses, believing it would protect their property from lightning strikes.

So there was considerable concern when such beliefs were severely criticised by the new Protestant clergy, and the churches stripped bare of all the precious things that the ordinary people valued most. In the reign of Mary, there was an attempt to restore Catholic forms of worship and ornament again, but so many features and objects from the church interiors had been sold or destroyed that they could never return to their former appearance. In any case, her reign was short. She was followed by Elizabeth I in 1558, who immediately ordained a return to the Protestant demand for the elimination of superstitious images and objects again.

The records in the Churchwardens' accounts for St Mary's throughout 1559 are quite repetitive – for example:

Item: 'paid to Molle for taking down the images'.
   'Paid to Cotes and But for breaking the images'.
   'Paid to Field and Towtlaye, for breaking down the altar, and carrying away the same'.

And in 1561, Molle and his apprentice were still busy removing the rood-loft where the great carved image of Christ on the Cross had hung. A stone-mason was removing all the holy-water stoups, and the painted image of St Christopher was finally defaced and obliterated.

There was clearly some conflict between the conservative parishioners who wished to retain some things as they had been and the more radical Puritans who wanted everything to be as Edward VI had previously ordained. Two Church Reeves at St Mary's, John Mannock and Edward Field (or Ffylld), objected to any features reminiscent of Popish Roman Catholicism. Parish accounts dated 30 April 1577, only a few months before the Black Dog event, refer to a conflict that had ensued between them and the church authorities in Norwich. They had taken it upon themselves to break down and remove the wooden partition between the chancel and the nave, and the authorities remonstrated that this was contrary to a commandment previously sent to the parishes. Partition screens were disapproved of by Puritans because they separated the altar and the clergy in the chancel from the nave where all the parishioners assembled. In addition, screens were often decorated with depictions of saints and angels, which had been banned during the reign of King Edward. Thomas Edwards, a Church Warden, records in the accounts that the screen should not have been vandalised because 'it was very comely and decently made, according to the Queen, her majesty's Laws', but either Field or Mannock has scrawled in the margin: 'Thomas Edwards here lies, for it was full of imagery not defaced!'

The outcome of this angry and violent controversy, which must have divided the parish into conflicting parties, was that Mannock and Field were dismissed from office, and replaced by two others more agreeable to the diocesan authority's view on church interiors. The disgraced pair were further condemned for 'their disobedience, and for the spoil that they before had made and done, contrary to the assent of the parishioners and commandments aforesaid'. In other words, it seems that they had broken or removed other furniture or items in the church.

With such bitter quarrels going on, and all the old, venerated and magical features finally being removed, the conclusion of many Bungay, and Blythburgh parishioners is obvious. Even their towns' most holy edifices were no longer secure from that great adversary, the Prince of Darkness, who held so powerful a grasp on their imagination. The churches and those who worshipped within them were at risk. And now it had happened: the Devil, in the form of a Black Dog had struck.

Although the apparition of a phantom Black Dog inside a church seems to be rare, there are some known precedents. In AD 857, a Bishop was celebrating mass during a thunderstorm at Treves, when the bell-tower was struck by lightning, darkness descended in the church, and an enormous black dog was seen running around the altar in circles. In 1341, a 'diabolical' dog entered the church at Messina, and proceeded to destroy the objects on the altar. But those events seem tame compared with what happened in Bungay and Blythburgh.

Phantom black dogs, and other phantom beasts have long been a part of folk tradition, and it seems likely that Suffolk people either knew of, or had experienced, frightening incidents connected with such Hell Hounds before.

In a situation such as occurred in the churches on 4 August, it's easy to imagine that when the church was plunged in darkness, and only fitfully illuminated in lightning flashes, the parishioners saw, at least in their mind's eye, the vengeful black dog which had formed part of their imaginations since childhood. They therefore believed that he was responsible for the deaths, injuries and damage. It would be a bit like having a character with a bad reputation living in the town. If a theft or murder happens which can't be easily explained it's soon blamed on the 'bad un' whether there's evidence to support the idea or not. When such a terrifying event happened within the sacred church – the supposed safe sanctuary for the entire community, it could only be caused by Satan, or one of his Demons, who, in the popular imagination, were often identified in the shape of a phantom black hound. 'Having the Devil on your back', and 'Having a black dog on your back', and being 'Dogged by bad luck', are all phrases making a connection between ill-fortune or ill-temper, dogs, and the Devil.

At the time, and ever since, particularly as civilisation has moved away from a supernatural to a more scientific understanding of the natural world, many have argued that there was no diabolic dog in the churches, it was just simple-minded people's imagination running riot. Other explanations have been offered as to why the event should be connected with a dog. The most frequent suggestion, is that there was *real* dog in the church, which, crazed by the storm and perhaps suffering from rabies, rushed about biting and injuring the cowering congregation.

It must be admitted that there were a lot of stray dogs around in towns throughout much of history, and until the twentieth century, when the RSPCA, police, and Dog Wardens, ensured that dogs found homeless were taken into care, their owners traced, or new homes found for them. Wild and stray dogs sometimes suffered from rabies, hunted in packs, and became ferocious through hunger, and could cause a threat to other animals or humans. They were also thought to be carriers of the Plague in the mediaeval period. As the doors of churches were frequently left open, allowing parishioners to go in and out during the day, dogs could easily slip in. They might go in looking for food or shelter, or for cool shade in the summer, or to follow a bitch on heat. In fact they became such a nuisance that parish records report methods of dealing with them. Bungay St Mary Churchwardens' accounts include payments at various times, for example:

1544 – Paid for a hespe of twine for the net at the church door.
1552 – Paid for stopping of the dogs out of the church.
1565 – Paid to James Johnson for driving dogs out of the church.

And similar payments are made throughout the year in 1577. In the following century, the altar rail was introduced especially to protect that sacred area of the church from becoming defiled by dogs. An edict, relating to the local churches, including Bungay, issued by Bishop Wren of Norwich, states: 'The rail (must) be made before the Communion Table, reaching from the North wall to the South wall, near one yard in height, so thick with pillars that dogs may not get in'.

Despite these arrangements, dogs often continued to get into the churches, and, quite apart from stray ones slipping in through the open doors, dogs were also brought into church services by their owners. Prominent and wealthy members of the community liked to have lap-dogs, or their hounds in church with them, and although the church authorities may have disapproved, they were often not in a position to forbid it.

So it seems likely that one or more dogs may have been in the church during that fateful morning of 4 August 1577, and it's certainly possible that a dog could have started howling and rushing about biting people. Dogs are usually terrified of loud noises, such as fireworks and thunder-claps, and might attack anybody near to them. The suggestion would make sense apart from two reasons. First, the deaths and injuries inflicted, so vividly described by Abraham Fleming, are consistent with being burned by fire, not by being savaged by an animal. In other words, caused by fire from a hell-hound, or by lightning, not by sharp teeth. Secondly, although Fleming describes members of the congregation being attacked, all the other contemporary records agree that it was only men in the belfry of the Bungay church who were victims. (Evidence for the event in Blythburgh has not survived). It's worth noting that the reason why John Fuller and Adam Walker were up there, was because it was believed the ringing of church bells during a thunderstorm would drive away the evil spirits in the air that were responsible for lighting flashes. Storms were greatly feared during the period when almost all buildings, apart from churches and rich-men's houses, were constructed of timber and thatch. A lightning strike could cause a whole town to be set alight within a few hours. Unfortunately, in their attempt to prevent a disaster, the two men were in the wrong place at the wrong time, and perished.

The point is that belfries in the mediaeval period were high up, and accessible only by ladders or steep staircases. It's very unlikely that a dog would either attempt, or be able, to get up into the belfry, and as already pointed out, if dogs were amongst the congregation they would only attack those around them, not make a long and difficult ascent especially to sniff out the two bell-ringers.

So the 'real dog' theory, doesn't stand up to investigation. The conclusion is that, if a dog was held responsible for the attacks on the parishioners and the building, it was a hell-hound in league with the Devil. There is no other explanation.

The legend is the most famous story connected with the two towns. The Bungay story is better known, because it forms the most prominent part of Abraham Fleming's account. However, Blythburgh church contains supposed evidence of the event, which Bungay St Mary's does not. The interior of the church door at Blythburgh is pitted with scorch marks, said to be caused by the Devilish Dog's claws, although the sceptical would attribute them to lightning flashes. Although Fleming reported that there were similar marks in the stonework of the Bungay church, 'and likewise in the church door, which (is) marvellously rent and torn, the marks as it were, of his claws or talons', no such evidence now exists. During the Great Fire of 1688, the church was badly damaged by parishioners insisting on dragging their possessions into the church for safety. Some of their bits of furniture were already

21. Black Dog weathervane, Bungay Market Place.

alight, thus setting fire to the church as well, and so it seems that the church door which contained the Dog claw marks, was either severely damaged or destroyed at that time.

In 1826, the account of the event written by Fleming was re-published by T & H. Rodd of London, and illustrated with a lively woodcut of the Black Dog racing along the aisle of St Mary's church. This edition also contained a verse narrative of the story, including the following lines:

> The church appeared a mass of flames,
> And while the storm did rage
> A black and fearful monster came
> All eyes he did engage.
> All down the church in midst of fire
> The Hellish monster flew
> And passing onward to the quire
> He many people slew.
>   Many were stricken to the ground
> Whereof they strangely died
> And many others there were found
> Wounded on every side.
> The church itself was rent and torn
> The clock in pieces broke,
> Two men who in the belfry sat
> Were killed upon the spot.

Rather an exaggerated account, but it helped to stimulate new interest in the event, and the verses were easy to memorise and recite, thus continuing to make the Black Dog disaster of 1577 even better known.

In Bungay the Black Dog has in recent years, been adopted as a symbol of town identity, although it's often asked – 'Why should the town wish to be so strongly identified with Satan's spawn?' In 1933 an image of him, with tongue hanging out, and tail waving, astride a curvy flash of lightning, was fashioned into an iron weather-vane and placed on a tall lighting-standard in the market place. He swings North, South, East, and West in all weathers, a reminder of his association with that dramatic thunder-storm, and remains a popular figure with both local people and tourists. The dog is also depicted in the town's coat of arms, granted in 1953, once again showing Bungay's individuality in choosing a Hell Hound instead of the more conventional lion crest. Other depictions of him can be found on the gates of the Council Office, on decorative wall plaques around the town, and in an embroidered wall-hanging, created by Mary Walker and a team of local embroiderers, displayed in the church. He has also given his name to an antiques shop, the football team, the running-club, the annual marathon, and a group of local artists. A spectre of terror in previous centuries, he has now become established as a rather endearing symbol of the town,

But only partially. Many people still claim to have frightening encounters with a ghostly black dog, usually when they are walking or travelling alone late at night. But is this the Black Dog, or another spectral hound that haunts East Anglia – the also infamous Black Shuck?

5

BLACK SHUCK AND THE OTHER BOGIE BEASTS

It's sometimes suggested that phantom hounds such as Black Shuck date back to Saxon times, and may have originated in stories told by Scandinavian tribes invading Britain after the Romans departed in the early fifth century.

Odin, king of the Norse gods, was believed to have become the ruler of the underworld when the pagan religions were suppressed by the new Christian priesthood. He became known as the Wild Huntsman, the Storm God, whose spectral pack of black hounds was said to haunt the doomed. Another legend concerns the Black Hound of Odin, left behind on earth when Odin departed to ethereal regions. He may be the prototype of spectral dogs, and it's easy to see the connection between the Storm God, his black hound, and the Bungay Black Dog. However, all this is speculation, because it's difficult to establish any clear link between Saxon mythology, and the accounts of spectral hounds which occur in Britain centuries later, and tend to be post Reformation.

East Anglia is particularly haunted by Black Dogs, and one possible connection with the Scandinavians, is that the name 'Shuck' is said to derive from the Anglo-Saxon word 'soucca' meaning Satan. However, Shuck could just be a regional variation of 'shaggy' or 'scruffy', which is generally how he is described. He is particularly associated with the coast stretching from Felixstowe to Hunstanton, as well as inland lanes, along the Peddars Way across Breckland, and on coastal paths from Cromer to Overstrand. There is a vivid description of him provided in Enid Porter's *Folklore of East Anglia*:

> He is a dog that walks regular. They call him Skeff, and his eyes are as big as saucers and blaze wi' fire. He is fair as big as a small wee pony, and his coat is all skeffy like a shaggy coat across, like an old sheep. He has a lane and a place out of which he come, and he vanish when he hev gone far enough.

This simple but graphic report is true to many descriptions of encounters with Shuck, who appears in particular spots and vanishes 'when he hev gone far enough'. Another vivid description comes from an old man who lived in Clopton Green in Suffolk. It was said he saw a 'Thing', with two great saucer eyes, on the road to Woolpit. It refused to budge out of his way, and then gradually grew bigger and bigger, and announced ' I shall want you within a week'. The night after, the man died. What a terrible vision to encounter just before death.

The Black Dog of Bungay and Blythburgh is often considered to be the same beast as Black Shuck, and connected with other spectral dogs in Britain. But there are reasons for suggesting that they may not be one and the same beast.

The Bungay Black Dog was seen only on one occasion, in two church interiors filled with congregations of people. He is particularly associated with a dramatic thunderstorm, violent injuries, deaths and damage. Black Shuck, however, is usually encountered by only one or two people, who are walking or travelling late at night, and see him often in deserted places such as coastal paths, empty streets or roads. He is also known as 'Old Shuck', or simply 'Shock', and described as:

A mischievous goblin, in the shape of a great black dog, the size of a calf, haunting highways and footpaths in the dark. Those who are so foolhardy as to encounter him, are sure to be at least thrown down and severely bruised, and it is well if they do not get their ankles sprained or broken; of which instances are recorded and believed.

This sounds much less terrifying and threatening than the Black Dog. Shuck is viewed as a harbinger of death or misfortune, rarely attacking or threatening those he encounters, although later, those who see him sometimes suffer accidents, or the illness or death of family close to them.

A typical account, in this case connected with a Norfolk sighting in the village of Winfarthing, records that one day, a local woman saw an unnaturally large dog approach her cottage. It padded up to her gate, and then suddenly disappeared. Her grandfather died shortly afterwards, and his unexpected death was attributed to the appearance of the dog. Many similar stories are told in the East Anglian region.

Often, though, Shuck seems to be of a kindly disposition, acting as a guide to accompany lone travellers safely to their destination. It seems unlikely although not impossible, that the Black Dog of Bungay will return to savage a church congregation, whereas Black Shuck has been, and no doubt will continue to be a regular night stalker of the Suffolk and other rural and coastal areas.

An example of Shuck as a quiet guide, was reported by Ernest Whiteland in 1938. He was returning from Bungay, along Bridge Street late one night, and as he got into Ditchingham, near the old Maltings (now being demolished for conversion to flats), he saw a black object, trotting along on the same side of the road, but slightly ahead of him. It was about ten yards away, and Mr Whiteland could see that it was about thirty inches in height, with a long black shaggy coat. Gradually it slowed down until it was level with him, and then suddenly vanished. Obviously it felt that the walker was in no need of his continued protection.

There are some connections between Black Shuck and witchcraft, although witches are more usually associated with black cats. During the witch-trials organised by Matthew Hopkins, the 'Witchfinder General' he arrested a couple from Halesworth, Thomas and Mary Everard. Thomas admitted that while he was serving as an apprentice, he was frightened by 'a black dog, like a water dog'. This reaffirms the connection between phantom dogs and water. Later, perhaps under the demon dog's influence, he suckled imps, and sent them to wreak mischief and malice on his neighbours by killing their deer and sheep. He and his wife also admitted to killing several people including their own grandchild.

Sometimes, like the spectral horses drawing phantom coaches in the region, Shuck is seen as headless. In this guise he was encountered several times at Barnby near Beccles in Suffolk, in the 1930's. His haunting spot was Water Bars, along the Lowestoft to Beccles Road, and an eye-witness describes him as 'big and black, but had no head. I put my hand down to coax the animal, but it went clean through it'. Another informant said 'The dog came up beside me, I put out my hand to touch it, but then it was gone'. In the same parish, he was encountered near where the old Hundred Stream flows under the road. The woman said that in around 1939, she was walking out with her sister to post a letter, and as she rounded the corner to the Post Office, they suddenly saw a big black dog. The woman thought that it was a neighbour's dog which had got loose, so she ran and tried to grab it, when in an instant it shrank to the size of a cat, and disappeared. This is the only known instance of anybody trying to grab a potentially dangerous phantom hound, and is not to be recommended!

A black dog has also been encountered at Blythburgh, more than four hundred years after the Black Dog's appearance in the church. The occurrence was in the autumn of 1973. A man described how he was laying a new sewer line across the marshes behind Blythburgh Church, and working alone at the time. He heard the sound of a dog panting, very close to his ear, and it was so frightening that he felt the hairs on his neck rise. He looked around but could see no sign of a dog anywhere. As he was not a local man, he had never heard of the Black Dog event in the church, but when he mentioned it to some friends later on, they said straight away 'Black Shuck!', and showed him an account of the local legend in a book. He added: 'According to the book the appearance of the dog is supposed to herald a death, and strangely enough, my youngest son died the following June…' It's a coincidence that the Dog was encountered so close to the church, but, because of the outdoor location, and the fact that the man was alone this is more likely to be a Black Shuck spectre, than another appearance of the rarer Bungay Dog.

Black dog phantoms have also been seen in Bungay and district, since the church appearance of 1577. However, the scarcity of sightings suggests that the creature occasionally seen is likely to be Shuck rather than the Bungay Dog. Mrs Hall, who lived in Broad Street, recalled seeing it on two occasions. In 1917, when she was a young girl, she was walking past Holy Trinity church, opposite St Mary's churchyard, when she saw a large black dog run from the Vicarage gate, across the road in front of her, and pass straight *through* the locked vestry door of Trinity church.

On the second occasion, in the early 1950's, she was walking a friend's dog in Nethergate Street, near her home, when she saw another large black dog run from Brandy Lane across the street, and disappear near the allotments at the end of the road near Outney Common. She recalled that on each occasion the beast had moved so swiftly that she couldn't make out its features, and that she had felt stone cold, and transfixed to the ground until the spectre had vanished.

Mrs A.M. Wilson was living in Beccles, near Bungay when she recounted the following story, in 1988:

This incident happened some sixty years ago, to my late father, and I heard the story from him more than once, without variation or embellishment. He was, it seems, born in the 'Chime Hours', and had always been very sensitive to atmosphere during the

22. Gargoyle, on the North wall of St Mary's church, designed to scare away evil spirits.

earlier part of his life. The incident took place at Earsham, just across the river from Bungay, one night shortly before Christmas, and very near to midnight.

My parents lived in Norwich, at the time, but my mother was having a few days at Earsham staying with her own parents who lived in the main part of the village. Father had arrived in Bungay shortly after 12 p.m. after finishing work in a Norwich bakery late. This left him to walk the last mile to the village as he had done several times previously when visiting. The only difference this time being that there was thick snow on the ground, and a bright clear moonlit sky.

As he approached the last of the row of cottages known as Temple Bar, he said he became aware of a horrible cold tingling sensation all over, and the feeling that his hair was standing 'on end'. At this point, he saw a large dog, probably black, come walking through the fence of the big private house known as 'The Elms', on his right, cross the road in front of him, a few feet away, and disappear through the wall, of the Rectory opposite. This he thought might have been a trick of moonlight through the trees, but, reaching the point where the dog had crossed his path, he found there was no sign whatsoever of any footprints, or other marks on the fresh snow.

At this point he panicked and ran fast as he could to my Granny's house in the main street. My granny verified this many years ago, by telling me that when she opened the door to him, he was shaking all over, and grey with fright.

At that time, my father had no knowledge whatsoever of local ghosts, Bungay Black Dogs, etc. having lived in the city all his life. By coincidence, roughly sixteen years later, after being bombed out of Norwich during the Second World War, we found ourselves living in the very cottage at Temple Bar that my father had been passing when he saw the dog; but never again did he see it, or get any weird feelings, even though we lived there for about eight years.

Another account, connected with the Earsham Street end of Bungay, was provided by Mrs M. Whitehead of Beccles:

My mother lived in Earsham Street, Bungay, with my elder sister, and I was at her bedside when she died in the early hours of the morning, on 11 January 1970. As she was not on the telephone, and I needed to inform the doctor of what had happened, I went to telephone from the kiosk outside the post-office.

As I went to cross Earsham Street, which was well-lit, I looked right, and saw this black dog in the middle of the road, running so fast towards Earsham, that its feet seemed barely to touch the ground. After passing me, it seemed to vanish, quite suddenly.

On relating this incident to my sister, on returning, she suggested that what I had seen must surely have been the Black Dog of Bungay!

This account is unusual, in that Mrs Whitehead saw the phantom dog shortly *after* her mother died, whereas more often, the beast is seen before a death or a catastrophe occurs. Nevertheless it makes the connection between Dog appearances and deaths, emphasising the usual frightening nature of phantom hounds.

Earsham is actually just across the river Waveney that borders Bungay from Norfolk, and Black Shuck has also been seen just across the border at Ditchingham another neighbouring village. He was seen by the distinguished local author, Sir Henry Rider Haggard, who lived at Ditchingham House. In *A Farmer's Year*, published in 1898, he mentions a belief persisting in that part of Norfolk and Suffolk, that 'the Devil is on rare occasions to be met with in these parts, and especially on Hollow Hill, in the concrete shape of the Black Dog of Bungay'. Hollow Hill is on the main road leading from Bungay to Norwich. Haggard was a friend of another celebrated author, Sir Arthur Conan Doyle. Doyle is perhaps best known for his spine-chilling tale, *The Hound of the Baskervilles*. It seems likely that Doyle heard tales of Black Shuck while he was recuperating from ill-health near the sea-side town of Cromer in Norfolk, from his friend Bertram Fletcher Robinson, a collector of local folklore; but he must also have heard tales about the Bungay Black Dog from Haggard, contributing to some of the descriptions in his Baskervilles novel.

Black dogs and similar phenomena are particularly associated with watery places. This is probably why they are frequently encountered in Norfolk and Suffolk, which have many river and marshy areas, and a long coastline.

The seaside town of Aldeburgh is associated with Black Shuck. His appearance and character is described by M.H. James, in *Bogie Tales of East Anglia*, published in 1891. At the north end of the town there is a walk across the common, and through a pine wood, skirting a mere, and leading to a sandy lane, with a kissing-gate at the end. It's at that spot that Black Shuck can be encountered after dark. James describes him as:

> the bogie, a large black dog, with fiery eyes, and a fierce appearance. Do not, however, be afraid of him, if you keep in the path that leads across the 'line' [railway], for all will be well, he will walk 'to heel', as a good dog should, and will only make you feel rather nervous by his odd silent trot; but, if you want to go the other way, he will show you what he thinks by an awful growling, he will stand in your path and show his teeth, he will snarl till you are almost paralysed with fear.

James goes on to describe how the beast never bites or barks, but he may grab hold of your clothes with his teeth if you try to thwart him. If you take the path he prefers, then he ceases to growl ferociously – instead he will follow 'to heel' and at the gate by the level-crossing, will sit down and watch you walk safely out of sight.

So this is Shuck as the protective guide-dog, who can be fierce, but rarely causes any real harm. Similarly a Shuck type dog has been seen at Walberswick near Southwold, and one story goes that during the Second World War, a coast-guard encountered him and was so scared that he drew his revolver and fired at him at close range. It seemed that the bullet had no physical impact, and the dog just vanished before his eyes. The dog has been seen there in more recent times, and also at Southwold on the Greens.

Another vivid story is connected with a Suffolk seaside town, probably Lowestoft, although the story is not clear. It was told by local fishermen and relates that a wealthy Italian, dark and swarthy looking, with much curly black hair, was living in the Lowestoft area. He became acquainted with a young fisher boy and asked if he would come into his employment as his page. The boy refused, but he remained friends with the Italian, and often romped with his black curly haired retriever on the beach. However, it was remarked that the dog and the Italian were never seen at the same time.

The Italian was obliged to return home to look after some affairs connected with his property, and left his dog behind in the care of the fisher-lad, The pair enjoyed

23. Lowestoft.

swimming in the sea each morning, and romping in the waves. One morning when the boy was enjoying his swim and about to return back to the beach, the dog suddenly attacked him clawing and biting, and driving him further and further out to sea. Staring into the dog's face, the boy was horrified to see its black furry features change into the face of its Italian owner! 'It bestowed upon him a hellish and triumphant grin, and then instantly resumed the form of the dog'.

It continued to maul the boy, but just as he felt he would sink beneath the waves, he managed to reach a nearby fishing-boat, where he was hauled aboard and revived. The dog dived beneath the waves, and neither he nor his Italian owner, were ever seen again. The fishermen were horrified by the bite and claw marks all over his body, and one of them recalled that there had been other incidents of young boys being drowned off Ness Point, and they too, had been found with claw and bite marks on their drowned bodies, one with his throat torn out. The story probably relates back to a mediaeval origin, because lycanthropy, the ability for some humans to transform themselves into half-man, half-wolf, was widely believed in, and feared at that time.

A black dog has also been seen at Dunwich by the coast, and the tradition is that if encountered, you should avert your eyes or close them tight to rob its power over you. You must never turn your back on it, or it will take advantage and wreak revenge. However, if it puts a curse on you, tell no-one, and if you remain silent about what you have seen and heard for a whole year afterwards, the curse on yourself and your family will be removed.

A variant phantom beast is the Gally Trot. It is the opposite of the black dogs, being white, about the size of a bullock, and rather shadowy in outline. It haunts a boggy pool called Bath Slough in the parish of Burgh, once again making the connection between phantom dogs and water. The name probably derives from *Gallibagger*, a bugbear, a word dating back to the sixteenth century used to describe a sort of hobgoblin to frighten naughty children. The word 'gally' often means to 'frighten', and it will be remembered that Black Shuck is often described as a sort of hobgoblin.

The Gally Trot seems to relate to the Faery Dog of Ireland. This creature is also about the size of a bullock, and although usually of a pale green colour, is sometimes white. It curls its tail over its back, and sometimes the tail is of a plaited style. It moves around in straight lines, occasionally emitting a loud howling bark, and the footprints it leaves are unusually large, about the size of a man's hand.

Gally Trots, like Black Shuck are shape-shifters, bogie beasts, meaning that they can disguise themselves in a variety of forms, including human. They are thus different from the Bungay Black Dog, who is always and only a dog. At Melton the bogie beast that haunts the area near the old Horse & Groom pub, has a donkey's head, and a smooth velvet hide like a calf, so very different from Shuck with his shaggy coat. 'Goodman' Kemp who tried to shoot and catch the beast in the early nineteenth century made a grab at it, whereupon it turned around and bit his hand, and vanished. Kemp bore the scars of the wound till his dying day.

Bogie beasts have different names in other parts of the country. Shuck is known as the Barguest, a dog-like goblin in the Yorkshire Dales. It is about the size of a small bear, of a yellowish colour, and with great round eyes like saucers. You must avoid its eye, or death is imminent, perhaps your own, or that of someone close to you. However, if the

24. The Galley-Trot.

25. Leiston Church.

Barguest pads behind you, and after a while, disappears your life is safe: if it continues to haunt you, you are definitely doomed.

There is also the Hazelrig Dunnie, a pony, in Northumberland, but a woolly sheep in Yorkshire, the Lackey Causey Calf in Lincolnshire, and in County Durham, the bogie can take the form of a white cat, or a rabbit, or a black or white dog.

The common at Walberswick near the Bell Inn, Newmarket heath near the race-course, and the headland north of Dunwich are other places in Suffolk where Black Shuck, or the Gally Trot may be seen.

Black dogs such as Shuck, are also connected with smuggling tales. Smuggling was rife along the Suffolk and Norfolk coasts in the eighteenth and nineteenth centuries. There were high taxes on imported goods such as spirits, tea, and tobacco, and as these 'luxury' items were popular at all levels of society, it was profitable to smuggle them into the country and sell them at more moderate prices.

Profitable, but dangerous. Customs and excise officers were stationed in various towns throughout the region, to detect and prevent any illicit trade, and those convicted faced the death penalty. Even those found harbouring pirates could be sentenced to death as felons. There were also generous rewards for 'informers' who were prepared to provide evidence of smuggling, leading to arrests; but, as smugglers were often violent and desperate men, many feared to reveal names in case they were viciously attacked or murdered. In 1745, a Beccles man suspected of 'ratting' on a smuggling gang, was dragged out of his bed at night, flogged, and tied naked to his horse. They then rode off with him, and, despite a £50 reward for information, he was never seen again, nor were his assailants detected.

Smugglers had to ensure that their activities went un-noticed as much as possible. People remained superstitious in the Georgian and Victorian periods, and so ghost stories were deliberately invented to frighten local residents into staying at home at night, when the smuggled goods were being brought ashore. This may be one explanation of why so many sightings of Black Shuck, and other spectral beasts, have been reported along the Suffolk and Norfolk coasts. Smugglers even went to the lengths of tying lanterns round dogs' necks, and letting them run through the darkness, so that anyone seeing them would immediately believe that Black Shuck was about.

The contraband goods, having been carried off the smugglers' cutters onto the shore, were often concealed locally and later conveyed to the towns. A gap in the cliffs between Pakefield and Kessingland, called Crazy Mary's Hole, was regularly used for carrying smuggled goods inland. Wherries were used to convey goods along the narrow waterways of the Waveney to towns such as Bungay and Beccles, and the city of Norwich was also a major destination. Farmers found it useful to get involved with smuggling to augment their incomes, and often provided the horses and wagons to convey goods. Tobacco, chests of tea, and barrels of brandy would be stacked in the wagon and then covered over with sticks or vegetables. In this way, the wagons could travel in broad daylight to deliver the commodities to their customers.

One farmer, Mark Butcher, who lived just across the river from Bungay at Earsham, had a large stone tomb built in All Saints churchyard, several years before his death. As it was rumoured that he was involved with smuggling activities, the authorities suspected that he might be using it to conceal smuggled brandy. He was taken to court, but insufficient evidence led to a Not Guilty verdict, and Butcher eventually died and

26. 'Guardian Angel', Blythburgh churchyard, scaring away evil spirits from the church.

was buried in the suspect tomb in 1809. The roads and lanes around Earsham are regularly associated with Black Dog sightings.

Blyford church was also used as a place for concealing smuggled goods, presumably with the knowledge of the parson, who, like Parson James Woodforde of Weston Longville in Norfolk, may himself have been a purchaser of illicit brandy and other items. It was said that barrels of grog were hidden under the pews, and even under the altar, presumably on the supposition that excise officers wouldn't dare to incriminate the clergy. The church at Blyford is close to the Queen's Head pub, used as the headquarters for smuggling activities, and it's rumoured that there was an underground passage connecting the two buildings. There were often battles between the smugglers and the excise men in this area, Blyford being a strategic inland village between Southwold on the coast and the towns of Halesworth, Beccles, and Bungay.

So the ghost stories were not just circulated by smugglers in the coastal regions but inland as well, and it would be interesting to discover whether there is a clear connection between reputedly haunted sites, and smuggling activities. Although Black Dog stories seem to have been the popular way of keeping people in their houses at night, smugglers sometimes used other methods as well, for example dressing up as phantom figures, and uttering strange scary noises.

Another illicit activity in the nineteenth century was the digging up of freshly buried bodies in the churchyards for sale to surgeons and medical students for research. The reason why many Georgian and Victorian tombstones still have iron railings around them, was to prevent such disturbances, and many memorials bear the inscription 'Let None Disturb His Bones'. So, just as smugglers invented stories to frighten people, so the grave-robbers also invented phantoms haunting churchyards so they could continue to plunder graves with less possibility of being detected.

Encounters with Black Shuck and other phantoms, are so varied, and have continued for such a long period, from at least the sixteenth century to the present day, that it would be absurd to argue that the incidents are largely the invention of smugglers and grave-robbers. Nevertheless, these men had a vested interest in keeping such stories alive in the popular imagination, and it may be that some of the accounts included in these pages originated from their activities.

6

SEASIDE SPOOKS AND
FRESHWATER MERMAIDS

Suffolk has an extensive area of coastline, stretching roughly from Oulton Broad to Felixstowe. There are many legends and ghost stories connected with coastal regions, and having recounted those that relate to Black Shuck, and other spectral beasts, this chapter deals with other strange encounters.

When we walk beside the sea, especially in the silence of early morning, or the twilight hour of sunset, we may often imagine that we can hear strange sounds murmuring from the waves – human voices, echoing gusts of laughter, ethereal music – but the sea at Dunwich has a different theme – the sound of church bells ringing out from drowned churches beneath the waves.

Dunwich was a prosperous port and town, or city, in the mediaeval period. Apart from many houses, shops, and taverns, it had a Franciscan friary, a leper-hospital, nine churches, and a variety of other ecclesiastical buildings.

It was a bigger town than Ipswich, but gradually the encroachment of the sea, particularly during periods of storms, high tides and high winds, caused the cliffs to crumble around the town's edges. Parts of it had already started to disappear at the time that Domesday Book was written in 1086, but it continued to expand and flourish as a great commercial centre, with a capacious natural harbour, well into the mediaeval period. But the sea continued its erosion of the cliffs, and, as the land receded, more and more of the buildings slid and toppled into the water.

John Kirby, writing in *The Suffolk Traveller*, 1764, records the names of all the churches thought to have been there, a Franciscan and a Dominican Friary, and that the churches of St Michael and St Bartholomew had been swallowed up by the sea by 1331. He concludes:

Whatever the ancient state of this place was, it is at present but a small Village, consisting of a few mean houses: it hath a mean market on Mondays and Fair on St James's Day, July 25th... it seems to have been at its Height in King Henry the Third's time... and to have declined also in that Reign, when the sea made so great a Breach here that the King wrote to the Barons of Suffolk to assist the Inhabitants in stopping it.

Kirby also records that in his day, 245 years ago, All Saints church was 'the only church now standing, and that in a mean condition'. By 1904, All Saints was so dangerously close to the cliff's edge, that it began to follow its former bretheren into the waves, and

27. The coast at Dunwich.

28. Woods near Dunwich.

the tower fell in 1919. Now, only a few gravestones in the churchyard survive to indicate that the church once stood nearby. The great city, as it was known, has shrunk from the size of a mighty oak to an acorn, and is now little more than a seaside hamlet. But it remains a popular resort, because it provides solitude and tranquillity away from the hubbub of more commercial centres, and its beach and woodland walks make it an ideal location for walkers and dog-owners.

On sunny days, there is a fine view across Sole Bay to Southwold, but it's at the close of the day, as the sun starts to sink and spread its coloured patterns over the water, that an air of enchantment conjures up visions of the lost city beneath the waves.

Human bones from the vanished church burial grounds are frequently found exposed on the beach. Local people say that the ghostly bells now ring out for a reason – to warn sailors that a storm is threatening, and that they should not take their boats out, or they may risk the same watery grave that the old town has suffered.

Nobody who walks there, and knows of the lost city, could fail to wish that a vision of its churches, houses, shops, and human activity, could be revealed, even if only for a moment – just to be there, just to see what it was like. And that adds to the perennial enchantment of the place, the tantalising awareness of what was there but is now hidden, and the possibility of hearing the bells ring out, as awe-inspiring as the sudden apparition of a human ghost. The 'mean' relic of Kirby's period, the ghostly relic of today, momentarily restored to its previous glory and prosperity again.

There is an excellent museum with displays relating to the town's past, but what an ideal site the area would make for an annual mediaeval fair, that could aim to recapture some of the spirit and colour of this most mysterious of Suffolk seaside locations.

Dunwich was founded, according to tradition, by St Felix of Burgundy, during his visit to Britain in the Saxon period in 632. Felixstowe, a prosperous port and town on the Suffolk coast, may also be named after the saint, and it too, has a tradition of bells ringing out from drowned portions of the old town beneath the waves: and the same relates to the smaller seaside resort of Aldeburgh.

Another story relating to Dunwich, although not connected with the sea, concerns the Barne family of Sotterley Hall. Sir George Barne, a Lord Mayor of London, came to live in the Dunwich area in 1552. His descendants lived at Sotterley Hall, about six miles north of Dunwich. In the Victorian period, a brother of the Lord of the Manor fell in love with a girl who lived near Grey Friars, just south of Dunwich, where the Barne family had a shooting-box. The lovers were forbidden to meet – presumably the girl was from a poorer family so any prospect of marriage was prohibited, and the disconsolate young man died of a broken heart. His ghost still wanders about the woodland paths of Dunwich, lamenting his fate.

Another ghost is the Squire himself, brother of the dejected lover. He rides about the same area on a fine Arab thoroughbred horse. Perhaps he's unable to rest peacefully in his grave because it was he who thwarted the plans of the young lovers and now regrets not having been more compassionate. The Barne family sold the Sotterley estate in 1947, and it's said that since that date the brothers are less seen looming around the area.

However, there is another ghost story connected with the family, that occurred in the early years of the twentieth century. John Baxter of Bungay, heard it from Jack Goddard a butcher of Lowestoft. Jack was a keen collector of moths. In order to prepare his specimens for display in their glass cases, he had to bake them to help preserve them, and this process tended to make their colours fade. Jack became expert at renewing their brightness with touches of watercolour paint, and John recalls that as a related hobby, he also became a fine water-colour artist.

On one particular occasion Jack and a friend went to Jay's Hill at Sotterley, on a night-time mission looking for more moths. The hill is quite steep, with wooded slopes on both sides. Jack spread out a sheet, with a lamp at the top of the hill to attract the moths to the bright light, and his friend did the same at the bottom of the slope, nearer the road. After about an hour or two, as they watched the moths fluttering around the trap, Jack heard the sound of a horse charging at full-tilt along the road, and thought it was strange to hear traffic on the road, for it was well after midnight. He therefore walked down to the road to investigate, and, just as he got to the verge, he suddenly felt the hot breath from a horse's nostrils, and the sound of terrified whinnying. Yet there was no sign of a horse anywhere,

Jack went back up the hill, and asked his friend if he had heard anything. No, he hadn't. Jack thought perhaps he had been imagining things, but the smell of the horses's breath and the sound of its cry still remained very vivid in his head.

A week or so later, he was having a pint with some friends in the local pub, when the conversation turned to the Barne family of Sotterley Hall. It seems that the two young sons had been going through a wild stage of their youth. One of the men described how the Barne's lads had been driving home, dead drunk in their pony and trap one night, and forcing the pony to fly along at break-neck speed. They were careering along the steep slope near Jay's Hill when the frightened animal lost his balance, he slipped, the trap keeled over and the youths were thrown out onto the road. At that very moment, another horse and cart was careering up behind them, and unable to stop, crashed over their bodies and both men were killed. The tragic incident had occurred on the very day, and only a few hours before Jack Goddard was out on the hill, hunting for moths.

At Walberswick, a ferry provides the crossing over the river Blythe that divides the town from the popular seaside resort of Southwold. As tourists wait for the ferry to arrive, they have sometimes observed an old man and a child also patiently waiting their turn to board. The ferryman, however, either fails to see them, or ignores them, and they are left still waiting silently and sadly as the boat rocks into motion. When passengers indignantly demand to know why they've been ignored, the ferryman replies 'O them! They're *allus* there. We don't take no notice o' them'.

It seems that they're the ghosts of a couple who took a ride on the ferry one day, when the boat capsized and they were thrown into the water and drowned. And forever after the lonely pair have continued to haunt the landing-stage, hoping for a safe journey home at last.

One of the strangest of all ghost stories connected with Suffolk is that concerning the wherry *Mayfly*. Every year on the 24 June, the *Mayfly* is cursed to return to Oulton Broad harbour with its cargo of lost souls, seeking to find the safe anchorage its passengers never reached in life.

The *Mayfly* was a trading wherry, mainly involved with carrying grain from local farms between Beccles and Yarmouth. Its skipper was Captain 'Blood' Stephenson, and it was owned by the prosperous Downey family. In June, 1851, it was carrying a

29. Waiting for the Walberswick Ferry.

very different sort of cargo, a chest full of gold pieces, which Mr Downey was having conveyed to his bank in Yarmouth. Also on board, to keep an eye on the family money, was his beautiful young daughter Millicent.

The crew on that particular day was Captain Stephenson, the chief mate, a deckhand, and a young boy, 'learning the ropes', as the saying goes, called Bert. Stephenson thought himself most fortunate in being entrusted with such a precious cargo, both the money and the young girl, and determined to steal them both. His plan was to make straight for a foreign port, where he couldn't easily be traced. A little while after the *Mayfly* set off, he revealed his wicked plan to the Mate, concerning the 'booty', and the 'beauty', both probably pronounced the same in his rough Suffolk dialect.

The Mate was horrified – he said he would take no part in such a scheme. An argument, and then a fight ensued, during which Stephenson toppled the mate overboard, and ignoring his cries for help, sailed speedily away, leaving him to drown.

After a time, ignoring the nearby coast, Stephenson began to reach the open sea, and then revealed his intentions to Millicent. If he was hoping for her willing co-operation he was badly mistaken. She struggled violently to resist his embraces, and so he forced her down below deck, and shut her up in the hold. Aware of what was going on, the deckhand intervened and tried to help her, whereupon another fight ensued, and the deckhand, too was soon thrown overboard. Bert also tried to remonstrate, but, just as he was about to seize Stephenson in a rugby-tackle, the Captain uttered a strangled gasp, and dropped dead at his feet in a pool of blood.

Millicent had managed to get out of the hold, and grabbing a kitchen knife with all her strength stabbed him through to the heart. She was so overcome by the horror of the situation, and the brutality of her action, that she fell down in a fit and was soon lying lifeless at the Captain's feet.

Only Bert was left alive on the doomed wherry. At daybreak, wishing to leave the scene of horror behind, he untied the dinghy from the deck, and set off on the open sea. Some time later he was rescued by a passing vessel, which took him to the nearest port of Plymouth.

For some time he lay ill, and convalescing in the hospital there, too feeble and distraught to be able to recall the terrible scenes he had lived through.

Eventually he returned to his home town of Oulton Broad, not far from Yarmouth. His former employer, Mr Downey took him back into his employment again. What had happened to the *Mayfly* still carrying the cargo of the chest of gold was never revealed, and maybe it eventually sank in stormy seas, or was captured by pirates.

Three years later, when Bert and Mr Downey were sitting by the harbour at Oulton one noonday in June enjoying a relaxing afternoon of fishing, Bert happened to look up – and was startled to see, sailing into the harbour, the wherry *Mayfly*. Both men gazed at it in astonishment. How could it return after a period of three years adrift at sea? But it was not the wherry as they remembered it. Now it glowed ghastly white with phosphorescence, moving in a stately, slow, and wraith like fashion over the calm waters of the harbour. As it drew ever closer they could see, standing at the wheel, a gleaming white skeleton – and – horror of horrors! there running across the deck, and screaming was Downey's daughter Millicent still pursued by the cruel skipper Stephenson.

And ever since then, its said that on the same day, and at the same time, the wherry *Mayfly* enacting the same horrible scene, continues to sail into Oulton harbour where the victims continue to seek the safe harbour they never found in life.

30. Oulton Broad.

31. Sutherland House, Southwold.

Another story connected with the sea is that concerning the naval battle of Sole Bay at Southwold in 1672. In the reign of Charles II, Britain was at war with the Dutch, resulting in various naval conflicts. Two important figures involved with naval strategy were the king's son, James, Duke of York, and Edward Montague, Earl of Sandwich. Montague lived at Shrubland Park, near Ipswich, so was a Suffolk man.

On the evening before the famous Sole Bay engagement, the Duke and Earl decided to get a comfortable night's sleep at the house called *Camels* in Southwold high street, which was being used as the headquarters for the military planning manoeuvres. The building was later re-named Sutherland House. An attractive sixteen-year-old girl, with auburn hair, was employed there as a maidservant. The Earl took a fancy to her, and after a bit of flirting and sweet-talking, persuaded her to spend the night with him in his bed-chamber, a spacious apartment on the first floor of the house. He obviously needed an enjoyable night's romp in order to distract his mind from the impending naval conflict.

No doubt, due to a rather energetic night's activity, the Earl overslept on the following morning, 28 May 1672, and arrived late on board the Royal James flagship. His officers were dismayed, and Prince James was furious. It was afterwards said that his unpunctuality was the reason why the British fleet failed to achieve a victory.

Their fleet consisted of seventy-one ships, mounting 4000 guns, and manned by 23,500 men, and they were supported by a French fleet as well, so it was a massive enterprise. Prince James was in command of the 'Red', and Montague in charge of the 'Blue'. As it happened, the Dutch fleet appeared unexpectedly early – the French panicked, and hurriedly deserted the operation, leaving the British to fight the Dutch fleet of sixty-one ships unaided.

It was a tremendous battle. The local inhabitants of Southwold and all the surrounding villages turned out to watch the onslaught from the cliff tops.

The fleets proved an equal match for each other, and the terrible and bloody battle resulted in major destruction of both fleets, thousands being killed, and eight hundred wounded men were eventually carried into Southwold for medical attention. In the end, neither side could claim the victory.

Montague was killed in action. Some time later his body was found washed up on Clacton beach, and identified by the signet ring he was wearing.

While the battle raged, the serving-maid, who it seems had fallen head-over-heels in love with the glamorous Earl, was gazing out of the upstairs window waiting anxiously for news of his return. When she learned the terrible truth that he had died in the battle, she was so distraught with grief, that she fell into a rapid decline, and died soon afterwards.

Its said that ever since she has haunted Sutherland House. Her pale anxious face appears at the upstairs window still watching for her lover's return, and inside, her footsteps can be heard pacing up and down the corridor outside the Earl's bedroom. These 'hauntings' are particularly frequent on the anniversary of the day of the battle, 28 May.

Joan Foreman, who visited the property in *c.* 1974 when she was gathering information for her book, *Haunted East Anglia*, records that the house has 'an indefinable sense of 'presence'; a concentration of energy, or a displacement of air, I do not know which', particularly in the area about six foot distant from the bedroom window where the

32. Gun Hill, Southwold.

girl's ghost still loiters. 'Whatever emotion was generated here the night before the naval battle appears to have remained'.

Another spirit haunting Southwold is on Gun Hill, a soldier, who can sometimes be seen standing next to one of the cannons mounted there. It's said he accidentally blew his own head off while firing the cannon, and he is sometimes seen as headless.

The Harbour Inn at Blackshore, near the estuary of the River Blyth, has also had ghostly happenings. An old service bell in the bar began to ring during the night, and as it hadn't been used for many years the landlord couldn't understand what had suddenly activated it. He was able to watch it while it was ringing, and although it continued vibrating, the old bell-pull rope remained absolutely motionless. The bell did the same thing one Christmas Eve while the landlord was serving a meal to his friends. The Inn is said to be haunted by an elderly gentleman, so perhaps he was feeling neglected and ringing to attract attention.

Mermaids are usually associated with the sea, beautiful but cruel maidens, who attract sailors by their lovely singing, and then entice them into the waves, and a watery death. But in fact the name 'mermaids' derives from an old English term 'mere' which can mean either the sea, or an inland pool or pond. Pools are still often referred to as meres, and there is a large one with this name in the centre of Diss in Norfolk.

The most famous association with sea-creatures in human shape in Suffolk is not a mermaid, but a merman connected with Orford Castle.

33. Orford Castle.

A twelfth century chronicler, Gervase of Tilbury claimed that a number of mermaids and merman inhabited the seas around the coast of Britain in the mediaeval period. Another chronicler, Ralph of Coggeshall, in *Chronicon Anglicanum*, describes how fishermen caught a merman, or 'wodewose', a wild man, in their nets, and carried the strange creature to nearby Orford Castle for the owner, Bartholomew de Glanville to examine. He was described as:

> naked, and was like a man in all his members, covered with hair and with a long shaggy beard. He eagerly ate whatever was brought to him but if it was raw he pressed it between his hands until at last all the juice was expelled. He would not talk, even when tortured and hung up by his feet. Brought into church, he showed no signs of reverence or belief. He sought his bed at sunset and always remained there until sunrise.

It's clear from this description that he was not actually a sea-creature like a mermaid because he didn't have a fish-tail. Perhaps he was not a fabulous creature at all, just a 'wild man' who preferred to be in the water rather than on land.

After a time of captivity in the castle dungeon the merman was permitted to spend time back in the sea, but carefully guarded. He seemed quite contented with his new way of life, but after a period of about two months, he disappeared under the water, evading his captors, and swam out further into the sea, and was never seen again.

According to Murray's *Handbook for Suffolk*, published in 1870, the *Wild Man of Orford* continued to haunt the village, but there seem to have been no sightings in recent times. The Wild Man was a sea-creature, but there are tales circulating in Suffolk about those mysterious and alluring maidens known as Freshwater Mermaids. They inhabit ponds, pools, and rivers, and are particularly associated with the River Gypping area of Suffolk which stretches from Ipswich to Needham Market, Stowmarket, and a few miles beyond. Beautiful to look at, they have long green tresses, with which they can entangle their victims, and it's easy to understand how their floating hair could be confused with the strands of water-weed found floating in pools and rivers.

Sea mermaids try to tempt sailors into the water to drown, but the cruel freshwater mermaids rise out of their watery homes when they see children approaching, and use all their wiles to make them plunge in. But do mermaids behave in this way out of spite and mischief, or because, lonely in their homes with only fish for company, they genuinely desire to share human company? No human has ever returned to tell.

James Bird who was born in Earl Stonham in 1788, and later moved to Yoxford where he died in 1839, remembered that when he was a child, his mother warned him against loitering near the edge of rivers or the mermaids might try to entice him in.

In *The Book of Days*, edited by Robert Chambers and published in 1863-4, a contributor recalled asking a child in Suffolk what he thought mermaids are, and he instantly replied – 'Them nasty things what crome you into the water!'. A 'crome' is a long handled rake with curved iron talons used in country districts.

A similar story comes from Rendlesham, in a letter published in the Ipswich Journal of 1877:

> When I was quite a child in 1814, we used to play at Rendlesham where there was a pond at one end with trees round it, the grass in early spring full of flowers. It was

34. Freshwater Mermaid.

always called the S pond being shaped like an S so drawn. If we went too near, our nursemaid would call out to us not to go near 'Lest the mermaid should come and "crome" us in'.

Sandra Welham, in a letter to the author, recalls that her mother-in-law, Kate Welham was a true Suffolk woman, born in Bacton near Stowmarket in *c.* 1908. She would regularly tell her grandson, Duncan – 'Don't go near the pond, there's an old mermaid living in there'. She later lost her husband when she was in her early fifties, and he was found drowned in the same pond. An open verdict was recorded, as it was not known whether it was an accident or manslaughter. Her daughter-in-law comments – 'I don't remember anyone saying anything about a mermaid being involved!'

Mrs Welham suggests, as others have done, that the tales may have been invented to discourage children from wandering too close to water, where they could easily topple in and drown. In country regions for centuries, one of the tasks given to children was to collect pails of water from the pools or streams, so warnings to 'be careful' coupled with scary stories about mermaids lunging at them with rakes, were entirely appropriate for their safety.

Mermaids are not actually 'ghosts', as they are not thought to be mortal creatures who have died and returned in spirit form. However, they certainly 'haunt' certain areas, and fulfil the criteria established for this book in that they can potentially be 'seen' or experienced by anybody visiting their habitats.

And they may actually be a manifestation of young women who have actually been drowned, and subsequently assumed mermaid form. At Fornham All Saints, near Bury St Edmunds, there are, or were, four mills, with pools of water known as the 'Mermaid Pits'. They are said to have been given that name because a girl, who was unhappily in love, drowned herself in one of them. Was she just a girl, who drowned, and afterwards haunted the pit? Or, following her death, did she change into the shape of a mermaid, and then, as is their way, forever after attempt to lure humans into the water to join her? Unless a long green tail as well as floating green tresses are seen in the pool, we shall never know.

Homersfield lies in the beautiful water meadow area between Harleston and Bungay. There is a ghost legend connected with the bridge there, which spans the River Waveney dividing the two counties of Norfolk and Suffolk. The original bridge was wooden, and then rebuilt in more recent centuries. The story goes that a ghost, or a devil was 'laid' under the bridge, that is, it was robbed of its magic powers so it could do no more mischief. There it will remain imprisoned for as long as the river continues to flow, because like witches and other malevolent creatures, such spirits cannot cross over running water.

Local people recalled that on one occasion, when some repairs were being made to the bridge, the ghost started uttering weird shrieks thinking it might be about to regain its liberty. It remains disappointed – at present! But with predictions that global warming may cause long periods of drought to occur, it may not be too long before he's free to vent his pent-up temper on local villagers.

The bridge was rebuilt in 1869 by Sir Shafto Adair, who lived nearby at Flixton Hall. The old supporting arches were retained but the rest was constructed from concrete, and it remains the oldest surviving concrete bridge in Britain. On the bridge today can be

35. Homersfield Bridge.

seen the heraldic crest of the Adair family, relating to the legend of the Bloody Hand. The information on the plaque reads:

> The legend of the design tells of a young ostler who was beaten so badly by his master that he died from the punishment. Before dying, the boy left a bloody handprint on the wall as a testimony of the assault. In those days the manslaughter of a servant was socially frowned upon and it was held that Adair should not go without some form of reproach. So it was that the sign of the red hand was added to the crest as a penance to commemorate the wicked deed.

As pointed out in *The Lore of the Land*, the 'Red Hand' is in fact the Red Hand of Ulster, the badge of baronetcy. The Adair family came to Flixton from Ballymena in County Antrim. It's thought that before the heraldic shield was more recently altered in its design, it only had three 'bloody' hands because the Adair family were permitted to reduce the mark of shame in succeeding generations. It's therefore odd that the design should now have four hands, but perhaps it was simply to serve as a reminder of the original tradition.

In this case it's unlikely that the savagely punished servant boy haunts the bridge area, but the story is included here to supplement the information provided on the plaque: and also, so that those who may hear the trapped spirit of the 'laid' ghost cry out, won't

36. Flixton Hall.

think he's the victim of the Suffolk branch of the Adair family, who were probably quite a pleasant lot.

Norfolk has a similar story concerning Sir Berney Brograve of Waxham Hall who also whipped a servant boy to death, and so the Berney family were obliged to display a 'Bloody Hand' as part of their crest. In fact, their family too, derived from Ireland, so the family tradition is also likely to be spurious.

If indeed the Adair family were guilty of such a brutal crime, the punishment they deserved occurred in the nineteenth century when their splendid mansion at Flixton was destroyed by fire. It was later rebuilt, but only survived until the 1950's when it was demolished, and now all that remains to indicate its former splendour are the wrought iron gates at the entrance to the park.

7

THE LAST GASP: HANGINGS, SUICIDES AND OTHER GRISLY ENDS

The Boy's or Gypsy's Grave, is just beyond Kentford about three miles from Newmarket, where the Chippenham/Moulton road crosses the main Newmarket road. Near the sign post is the grave, and it's easy to spot because it's regularly adorned with floral tributes, said to be brought by gypsies who wish to commemorate the tragic death of one of their own kin.

The site is haunted, and tales are told of cyclists who are mysteriously forced by some strange unseen power, to dismount as they near the spot.

There are various stories connected with the boy who is buried there. Lillias Rider Haggard in *Norfolk Life*, published in 1943, dates the burial back to the seventeenth century. A young boy was tending his master's flock of sheep, in the fields not far from the cross-roads. At night, as usual, he led them into their fold for safety and sleep, but as he counted them in, he noticed that one was missing. Although he searched high and low, he was unable to find it. He became so full of remorse, and fear of how he could explain the loss to his master, that he hanged himself from a tree by the side of the road. Another version of the story identifies the boy as being a gypsy, which is why gypsy families today like to keep the site neat, and bright with flowers.

A superstition connected with the grave is that sometimes, coloured ribbons were tied to the osiers surrounding the grave, and these are supposed to indicate the colours worn by the jockeys who will win the next big races at Newmarket. So punters would visit the grave to check the ribbons before putting their money on a particular horse and jockey.

The grave has been a local landmark for a long time, as the story of the boy's death attracted interest and sympathy. It seems to have become a semi-official site in the 1970's, when a wooden or wire railing was provided around it, and the site marked with a cross and the inscription: 'Joseph – the Unknown Gypsy Boy. Rest in Peace'.

No recent stories have circulated about the ghost of the boy hovering there, but it must be his supernatural aura which compels cyclists to dismount and approach his grave. As a suicide, he was not permitted to be buried in consecrated ground in a churchyard, but now he is frequently and affectionately remembered in his roadside shrine.

The picnic site known as 'Toby's Walks', near the A12 south of Blythburgh, is associated with 'Black Toby'. The paths between the gorse-bushes on this piece of common land are where his ghost is said to wander, lamenting his fate. Tobias Gill was a black drummer in the regiment of dragoons commanded by Sir Robert Riches. They

37. The Gypsy's Grave, near Newmarket.

38. Toby's Walks, Suffolk County Council picnic site, Blythburgh.

The Ghostly Tale

Local legend tells of a young soldier called Tobias Gill, who was camping at Blythburgh. One evening Toby became drunk and wandered over the heathland, where he met a young girl called Ann Blakemore. Next morning Ann was found dead on the walks. Toby was arrested for the murder and hanged at Toby's Walks.

The gibbet, used for the hanging, stood for 50 years. When it eventually fell to pieces, a thatcher used the nails to make a thatching comb. The story tells of Toby still walking over the heath, giving his name to this picnic site.

Suffolk County Council
Environment and Transport

39. Toby's Walks, Information plaque, Suffolk County Council.

40. Deadmen's Corner, Yoxford.

were quartered at Blythburgh for a week in 1750. The story goes that one evening Tobias had a lot to drink in the local pub, and stumbled back to his camp, blind drunk, across the common. On the way, he encountered a servant girl, Ann Blakemore, and on the following morning he was found lying on the ground, still dead drunk, and her body was lying on the grass beside him.

It was surmised that he had attempted to kiss her, she had resisted, he had then forced himself upon her, raped, and murdered her. Late at night, in an isolated spot, nobody would have heard her cries for help.

Tobias was tried and convicted of the murder at Ipswich Assizes. His body was then hanged in chains at the crossroads near where the crime had been committed. In those days, hanged criminals were usually exposed on the public highways as a warning to others until their bodies had completely rotted away, with only the skeleton left.

So it's hardly surprising that he is still thought to haunt the area. He also haunts the local churchyard where he is perhaps wandering to seek Christian forgiveness for his crime. A phantom hearse can sometimes be seen in the vicinity. When Tobias was convicted by the judge, he requested that he might be dragged at the end of a mail-coach by a rope, rather than being hanged on the gallows. The judge refused, and it's now thought that the phantom coach bearing a hearse, and drawn by four headless horses, is driven by Tobias himself, still bearing a grudge about his rejected plea.

The 'Toby's Walks' picnic site is not far from the haunted Blythburgh church, and the haunted White Hart inn. There is an information board at the site, telling the story about Tobias Gill's connection with the gorse-covered common area nearby. It seems a bit macabre to create a family picnic site near a spot connected with a brutal rape and murder, and the name 'Toby's Walks' suggests not just the pathway he walked along on that fateful night in 1750, but that he is still looming around there today. But only after dark, when most picnic-ing families will have gone home.

Dead Men's Corner at Yoxford, another cross-roads area, is thought to be the burial site of either a pair of criminals or a pair of suicides.

Letters about the site were published in the *East Anglian Magazine*, in the May and September issues in 1952. The stories that had been circulating involved either suicides, gypsies hanged for sheep stealing, or ghosts from nearby Darsham Rectory. Some locals affirmed that there was only one grave, containing the bodies of two men who had killed each other in a duel.

One of the correspondents recorded that the graves had been freshly built up and turfed about fifty years previously by East Suffolk County Council. The workmen told her that it was exactly a century since the burials had taken place, and another local informed her that the grave contained two suicides.

A further correspondent wrote, confirming that the graves were being maintained by Council workers, but his version of the burials was that, in the early nineteenth century two men had quarrelled, one shot the other, and then, either from fear or remorse, hanged himself from an oak-tree nearby.

An East Suffolk County Council Roads Supervisor informed the Editor of the *East Anglian*, that the graves had actually been tended by a retired roadman until about 1942. Some other workmen who had come to investigate a subsidence in the road nearby had dug into the grave, and discovered human bones, so the burial tradition seems to have been confirmed. During the Second World War, the site had been covered

41. Dead man hanging.

42. Frederick Rolfe.

by sugar-beet, and later obscured by the frequent passage of tractors going in and out of the nearby field, and since then, the grave had been no longer visible. The authors of *The Lore of the Land* conclude that the crossroads site suggests suicides rather than criminals such as sheep-stealers.

Locals have reported that it is a spot much feared, as likely to be haunted by the ghosts of the dead men buried there. Recent conversations with locals in the pub nearby, revealed that the road, (where an Antiques centre is now situated) continues to have an eerie atmosphere.

Kesgrave, between Ipswich and Woodbridge, is also the haunt of a suicide. Dobb's Lane is a track leading to what is known as 'Dobb's Grave'. Dobb was a shepherd who hanged himself at Kesgrave Hall Farm. Could it be because he had lost one of his master's sheep? There seems to be a suspiciously high number of shepherds hanging themselves in Suffolk, but with only sheep for company all day, it's hardly surprising. Like other suicides, poor Dobbs was buried in un-consecrated ground near the cross-roads, and his grave is marked by a concrete headstone. Those who wander near the spot at night may hear him bleating. One evening, not so many years ago, a group of rowdy lads decided to have a go at digging the grave to see what it contained. They eventually dug up human bones, proving that the story of a burial there was based on fact. It's said that one of the lads involved, took a tooth as a trophy, which he wears on a watch-chain. But what if, one dark night, Dobbs returns to claim it back?

In Bungay, Frederick Rolfe's disturbed spirit may still hang around either the cemetery where he's buried, or Nethergate Street, where his life ended. Rolfe was the self styled 'King of the Norfolk Poachers', and he told his own life story in *I Walked by Night*, edited by Lillias Rider Haggard, and published in 1935. She writes in the introduction to his autobiography:

> What is written here was born of an old man's loneliness, as he sat in a little cottage perched high on a hill, overlooking the Waveney Valley, with no company but his dog. The life that he loved had passed him by. As he puts it, 'some said I had given up the game – but the game gave me up', so, to pass the time, he took to writing down his memories in a penny exercise book.

That penny exercise book is on display in Bungay Museum, together with a couple of Rolfe's poaching guns, one of which conveniently folds into two halves so he could quickly shove it down his trouser leg if he saw a land-owner or policeman approaching.

Rolfe was born and lived in north west Norfolk before moving to the Bungay area in later life. He held various jobs, including those of house-boy, shepherd, horsebreaker, mill hand, gamekeeper, and rat-catcher to the army troops. While still a boy, he was sentenced to a month's imprisonment at Norwich Castle for snaring a rabbit, and forced to work the treadmill. Like many men living in rural areas during periods of acute economic depression, he was forced into poaching in order to provide food for his wife and children. For him, it subsequently became a preferred way of life. Rolfe was inevitably often in trouble with the law, and served periods in a prison cell, but he was a quick-witted and cunning character, and, more often than not, managed to outwit the local 'bobbies' on the track of his midnight poaching manoeuvres. Having thankfully escaped detection once again, he could relax and have a laugh with his mates in his local pub, the Chequers in Bridge Street.

However, when he was in his seventies, he suffered increasing ill-health and underwent a severe operation in the Norwich hospital. His criminal life as a poacher was drawing to a close, but he became involved in a much more sinister incident. The knowledge, that if this new crime was revealed, he could face a long prison sentence – possibly a life-sentence – preyed heavily on his mind.

Les Knowles lived in a cottage next door to where Rolfe lodged with a Mrs Redgrave, in Nethergate Street. Les was aged about five in 1938, the year Rolfe died. He remembers him as a heavily built man, and to a child, rather a frightening character. Les attended the Primary School, and on his way home he liked to take a quick short-cut through the stable doors and sheds of the Maltings in Nethergate Street, to his house. He recalls the particular occasion when he arrived home, and his mother asked, 'However did you get that bruise on your forehead? Have you been fighting?'. He replied, 'No, Mum, Mr Rolfe kicked me!'.

His mother thought he was telling fibs, as there was no way their neighbour would kick a child. But when her husband returned home, and she told him what Les had said, and the boy persisted with his story, his father said: 'Right – I'll soon get this sorted out. I'll go straight round to Mr Rolfe and ask him!'

When he called next door, Mrs Redgrave said that Rolfe had gone out that morning, and hadn't yet come home. As the afternoon drew on she started to get worried, and eventually, a search was made. He was found, hanging from a beam in the Malting's, having committed suicide. Young Les had run straight into the dead-man's swinging feet as he raced through the stables, and that was how he had received the nasty bruise on his face.

The inquest on the dead man was recorded in the *Beccles & Bungay Journal*, on 26 March 1938:

Sitting at St Mary's Mission Hall, Bungay... the Coroner was told the story of the tragic end of Frederick Rolfe... described as a retired warrener and old-age pensioner. He was a widower.

Mrs Jessie Redgrave, a widow living at 15, Nethergate street, Bungay, said deceased had lodged there for the past fourteen years. On Wednesday, she came downstairs at about 7.45 am and saw a note lying on the living-room table. She was unable to read, so she took it to her daughter upstairs. It was in deceased's hand-writing, and after hearing the contents read, she sent it to Sergt. Sawyer [the local police-officer]. At about 3.30 pm the same day she was told by the Sergeant that Rolfe was found hanging in a shed at 1, Nethergate Street. Deceased had been worried since Monday night, when she had to talk to him concerning a matter of a rather serious nature. On Tuesday, Rolfe told her he knew the way out of the trouble. She last saw him alive at 9.45 pm that day, when he went to bed. He stopped at the door and said 'Goodnight, mother. This is the last time I shall bid you goodnight'. She told him not to be so silly. After that she heard no more of him. He had enjoyed good health recently.

P.C. Dunnett said that on Wednesday, he went with Sergt. Sawyer to look for deceased. At 3.35 pm he went to premises in Nethergate Street, and in a disused meal-house saw Rolfe hanging by a piece of wire from a beam. They released Rolfe, who had been dead for some hours. He was fully dressed and his trilby hat was lying nearby.

P.S. Sawyer said it was evident that the hanging was a determined effort. There was practically nothing of value on the body, but in a leather wallet in the jacket pocket he found a note [produced] which he knew to be in Rolfe's handwriting. This note was not read out to the Coroner.

Witness added that in the course of his duties, he had recently had occasion to interview Rolfe.

The Coroner said it was quite clear that Rolfe took his own life. He returned a verdict that death was due to asphyxiation by hanging, self-inflicted, whilst the balance of his mind was disturbed.

It was clear that worry about the discovery of his crime had preyed on Rolfe's mind, and he had dealt with it in his own way. Suicide is often called the 'easiest way out', but taking one's own life can never be an easy decision. It certainly wasn't for Rolfe.

I Walked by Night was illustrated by the celebrated East Anglian artist Edward Seago. The last illustration, forming the tail-piece to Rolfe's narrative, is a drawing of a steel animal trap. Such cruel weapons, inflicting slow torture and death on dumb creatures who can't protect themselves were used on a daily basis by Rolfe during his poaching career. It's ironic, that in the end, a wire snare was to be the instrument of his own death.

Following the inquest, he was buried in unconsecrated ground on the north side of Bungay cemetery in an un-marked grave. Since then, his autobiography, *I Walked By Night* has become an East Anglian classic. Some say he continues to 'Walk by Night' in Bungay.

In the seaside resort of Lowestoft, a ghost is rumoured to haunt the dock area of the North Quay. Two men, Edward Rollahide and George Turner, were working as building labourers on the construction of the North Quay West in 1921. During a break, they were enjoying a friendly game of cards when an argument started between them. Rollahide became so furious, that he picked up an axe standing nearby, and chased Turner round the building site with it, lunging at him as he ran. He then tripped, and fell into a pit of wet cement. With a shriek of horror he disappeared beneath the surface, and was never seen again.

Some time later, when George Turner was returning home from a night out in the local pub, he was walking past the North Quay, when he saw the ghostly shadow of Rollahide approaching him out of the darkness. He then started lunging at him again, cursing and screaming, just as he had done on the day of his death. Being a ghost his attack could make little impact, and he finally disappeared, still muttering, through a wall.

Turner was so shocked by this frightening apparition, that he fell ill, and died soon afterwards. The ghost, it is said, has been witnessed on subsequent occasions, so Rollahide was not just returning to revenge himself on Turner, but continues haunting the spot to complain about the unlucky accident of his death.

Letheringham water-mill near Wickham Market is on an ancient site, for a mill is recorded there in Domesday Book. The mill has been re-built over the centuries, and the existing building dates from 1740. In the previous century, in 1696, the miller John Bullard, and his son were busy working on their accounts one day, when one of their temporary employees, a journeyman, Jonah Snell rushed in and murdered them with an

43. Lowestoft.

axe. It's not clear whether it was revenge for some grievance he held against them, or just that he was after the money they were counting. He then tied ropes around them and left them hanging from a beam in the roof.

Snell was later arrested, and taken to court at Wickham Market where he was convicted of the murders. He was then hanged in public on the gibbet at Potsford, and left there to be exposed until his body had been pecked away by the birds.

In Potsford Wood, near the B1078 road, some tree-felling was being organised in 1958, when the remains of the old gibbet were discovered there. It's thought to be the same gibbet on which Snell was executed. It was decided to re-build it, and it now bears a plaque commemorating its use and associations. The site around the gibbet is said to still be haunted by Jonah Snell.

8

HAUNTED HOUSES

There are a number of ghostly hauntings relating mainly to Georgian and Victorian houses in Suffolk. Boulge Hall near Woodbridge was demolished in the 1950's, but had a previous history of ghostly goings-on, and some of the apparitions may still hover around the site. An extensive Georgian mansion, it was particularly associated with the wealthy FitzGerald family, of whom the most celebrated member is the poet Edward FitzGerald, (translator of the *Rubaiyat of Omar Khayaam)* who inhabited it in the Victorian period.

But in the Georgian period it was occupied by Mrs Short, so notorious for her vicious temper that she became nicknamed 'The Queen of Hell'.

She inherited the property following the death of her second husband, William Whitby in 1792. Later on, she married Henry Haggard, who had been a Lieutenant-Colonel in the Royal Dragoons, and subsequently assumed the name of Short, perhaps in connection with some inheritance.

Due to Mrs Short's quarrelsome nature, the marriage was a stormy one, and the couple were frequently involved in violent arguments. At last their marriage became so intolerable that Mrs Short had a cottage built in the grounds of the Hall so she need see as little of her husband as possible. It was the same cottage later occupied by Edward FitzGerald, who needed peace and quiet for his writing, and also wished to see as little of *his* family as possible.

Her nephew described her flying into a terrible rage on New Year's Day in 1800. She had another violent quarrel with her husband at the Hall, when it seems that she may have threatened him with a knife. She had to be restrained by four men, and was locked in one of the rooms for the safety of the household. She attempted to break the door down, in order to escape, and smashed the windows, and vowed she'd burn the place down if she wasn't freed immediately. It seems there was some truth in her threats, for later on a hole was found burnt in the floor in the middle of the room, as if she had torched it with a candle or glowing coals from the fire.

This episode is also said to relate to stories of bloodstains on the floor, and the murder of a gentleman, by Mrs Short, but that may be just an exaggerated version of what actually occurred. The 'haunting' tradition was related in 1893 by Mr Redstone, who was an English master at Woodbridge Grammar School. His account was that, having murdered somebody at the Hall, she now appears at night driving through the gates into the park, in a phantom carriage, drawn by a pair of headless horses. She wears a

44. The Farmer's Ghost.

silk dress, and can be seen due to a lamp shining from the vehicle. He added that about three years previously, i.e. in 1890, she entered the Hall, and, terrified a young servant girl who was lying in bed. She described how the ghost of Mrs Short loomed up to her, and pulled the clothes off the bed, and she could feel her 'breath like a wolf upon her'. If the lady was known as the Queen of Hell in her lifetime, it's not surprising that she was rumoured to return from the regions of Hell after her death, to haunt the house which had been filled with her fiery temper and which she had threatened to burn down.

Mrs Short's eccentricity is confirmed by the FitGerald family, who purchased the estate in the early part of the nineteenth century. They couldn't inhabit the house immediately because, following her husband's death, she remained the sitting tenant. As it happened they couldn't take possession until thirty five years after they purchased it, and so occupied nearby Bredfield Hall. Edward FitzGerald's biographer records: the family 'knew that Mrs Short was not an easy woman, and Bredfield was a handy vantage point from which to keep an eye on her and Boulge'. Obviously they had heard about her fire-raising threats and murderous tendencies in the village!

The phantom coach story is also connected with the FitzGerald family, in particular John, Edward's brother. Edward believed that they all had 'tainted blood', which explained their melancholy dispositions and eccentricities, but John was the most eccentric of them all. He was very religious, and became a lay preacher, a role for which he was not well suited because he had a bad habit of 'sissing' or whistling in his speech, that alternated with a clicking of his teeth, and seemed even more exaggerated when he was in the pulpit. He used to hold services at a lunatic asylum near Boulge, where all the inmates took to imitating his strange noises while he preached. During his preaching he would also abstractedly remove all the contents from his pockets, and lay them out on the lectern, and then remove his shoes and socks which he would proceed to examine carefully without ceasing in his orations. He was heavily built, weighing eighteen stone, and also had a habit of gesticulating with a lighted candle, causing hot wax to be spattered all over his congregation in the front pews.

On the death of his father in 1852, John inherited the Boulge estate, developed increasingly odd behaviour, and eventually died in 1879. Thereafter it was rumoured that it was he who haunted the Hall. At midnight, a phantom coach drawn by headless horses, and with a headless groom would arrive at the entrance gates by the lodge-house. It was there to collect John FitzGerald, and the reason why he is thought to have continued to haunt the place must be due to his eccentric behaviour during his life. One of his oddities was that if he had been away on a visit, he would arrive at the Bull coaching inn, about three miles from the Hall, ignore the coach that was waiting to collect him, order a fly instead, and then proceed to walk home, with both the carriage and the fly following behind him. Upon arrival, he complained at having to pay for a vehicle that he hadn't used. This may explain why his ghost is associated with a waiting coach, in which he is never actually seen to travel.

Clopton Hall is not far from Boulge. In 1928, it was bought by Justin Brooke, who describes his life there in *Suffolk Prospect*, published in 1963. Brooke also bought the farmhouse which adjoined the Hall, and which several years previously had been occupied by a prosperous farmer. He had died a bachelor, and local gossip muttered that he had accrued a fortune that was probably hidden in a chest somewhere in the house or grounds.

Brooke was told by a local man, that, as a boy he had lived at the farmhouse which his father occupied as a farm worker after the batchelor farmer had died. One night when the boy was sleeping in his bed, he was suddenly woken by a tall figure, who silently beckoned him to get up, and follow him. The boy was terrified, and shouted 'NO! Go away'. The figure disappeared. The next night, it appeared again, drew back the boy's bedclothes and again urged him to rise and follow. Once again the boy shouted 'Go away', and hid back under the blankets. On the third night, the ghostly figure pulled all the clothes right off the bed, but the boy shouted 'GO AWAY, DAMN YOU!', so vehemently, that the ghost disappeared immediately and was never seen again.

The boy was an old man by the time he told Justin Brooke this story. He said that, with hindsight, he regretted not having obeyed the midnight phantom, and followed him, for perhaps it was the ghost of the farmer who wished to lead him to where his chest of treasure lay hidden. 'If I had done so', he lamented, 'I could have grown up to become a fine gentleman and would never have had to work for my living as I have done'.

Such stories as this where ghosts try to reveal secrets to the living are fairly common in folklore, but it seems very seldom that the recipients gain any benefit from the information.

Another tale of hidden treasure is connected with Dallinghoo, where a man buried his fortune under a gatepost. The exact location seems to have been forgotten, unfortunately, but the owner haunts the spot nearby, perhaps to guard it, perhaps to reveal it to some brave human who's prepared to stay and listen to his ghostly tale. So hang around the village around midnight, and you could strike lucky!

Dallinghoo is also haunted by a 'footless' ghost, the Widow Shawe who had committed suicide by slitting her throat. She's been seen flitting about the local lanes, floating above the ground as if she had no feet to walk upon. No explanation has been provided for her lack of feet. Perhaps it's because, as she wears long skirts, her feet are concealed, and as most ghosts are said to glide or hover, rather than walk, she never seems to plant her feet firmly on the ground as humans do. Still, she can probably move pretty fast if you attempt to run after her.

Hintlesham Hall is a few miles distant from Ipswich. Built originally of Tudor red brick, it was renovated in the eighteenth century, and provided with stone facings. In 1747 it was acquired by Sir Richard Lloyd and was subsequently inherited by his son, and then his grandson, both of whom were confusingly christened with the same name of Richard Savage Lloyd.

One of the Richard Savage Lloyd's married twice. His son by his first marriage was badly treated by his second wife, who obviously resented the child. She neglected him to the extent that he eventually died of starvation. As a result of this tragic death, the house is said to be haunted, particularly the areas of the main staircase and library. On occasion, the library doors have swung open, as though pushed by a human hand, and then they snap shut again. Perhaps it's the ghost of the starved child, come to plead for food from his cruel stepmother, but being turned abruptly away.

A dummy figure was made of the boy after his death, perhaps a funeral effigy made of wax. Such commemorative and decorative figures were popular in the Georgian period. It was placed on the great staircase, with a protective curtain in front of it, drawn back when visitors were expected. The figure became known as The Luck of Hintlesham, and it was believed that if it was ever removed or destroyed, the owners of the house would suffer misfortune. Mary Lewes, who knew the family living in the house in the late nineteenth century recorded in her book *Stranger Than Fiction*, published in 1911, that on one occasion the effigy was removed from the staircase, because a dance was being held on that occasion. During the night, a minor earthquake occurred on the site, and part of the house collapsed. She actually refers to the figure as being a girl rather than a boy, but in the Georgian and Victorian periods, both sexes tended to be dressed in girlish clothes.

Oulton Manor House was built in the sixteenth century. During the reign of George II (1727-60), the house was owned by a 'roistering' squire, who loved hunting, gambolling, wine, women, and song. His wife obviously felt neglected, and one day the squire returned home to discover her in bed with her lover, a young army officer. A quarrel, and then a fight ensued between the two men. The squire struck the officer in the face, whereupon the impetuous officer grabbed his sword, and stabbed the squire clean through the heart.

Knowing that the crime would very soon be discovered, the couple swiftly packed all her jewellery, and as much money as they could lay hands on, and made a quick get away. They left behind the squire's daughter, who would have discovered her father's dead body soon afterwards. As her mother was missing, she could not know that she was involved in the incident, for it may have been that she had been abducted by the murderer who caused her husband's death.

The daughter continued to live at the Hall, and some years later became engaged to a local farmer. On the eve of their wedding, they were sitting together in the house on a bleak November night, when they heard the sound of a carriage draw up outside on the drive. Going to the door, they saw a black funeral carriage, drawn by black horses, and attended by servants wearing black mourning clothes. Seated inside the coach was the girl's mother, and, in her hand, she was holding a silver chalice containing poison. She had arrived to kidnap her daughter, having been living in dread that the girl might know the truth about her father's murder. Masked men rushed into the Hall, stabbed the farmer, and carried off the screaming girl in the carriage. It rattled away down the drive at break-neck speed, and neither of the occupants were ever seen in Suffolk again.

The story affirms that the girl was indeed poisoned by her mother, and was buried in a convent cemetery at Namur in Belgium. For ever afterwards it's been believed that the house is haunted, and on certain nights, a ghostly lady bearing a poisoned chalice is seen wandering in the grounds. A huntsman and hounds also appear, the ghost of the squire, who, it was related, had been out hunting on the day he was murdered.

Thorington Hall, west of Ipswich, is haunted by the 'Brown Lady', a girl who wears a brown dress with a cord tied around the waist. In the 1930s she was seen by the caretakers who lived in the house, Fred and Elizabeth Burton. She was standing at the top of the stairs, at dusk, and when she saw Fred looking at her, she raised her hand to her mouth in surprise, and disappeared. Her footsteps have been heard hurrying along the upstairs corridor, and also some heavier footsteps – perhaps those of a ghostly assailant who had threatened or murdered the girl? The Hall has been owned by the National Trust since 1941.

Reydon Hall, opposite the turning to Frostenham, on the Wangford to Reydon Road, is another property haunted by a phantom coach. Like the others already mentioned,

45. Roos Hall, near Beccles.

it's drawn by headless horses, and seated inside is a local squire, who committed some hideous crime and is doomed to travel the area. It's not known whether he's associated with Reydon Hall itself.

This spot can frighten horses, who are sensitive to supernatural phenomena, and, during the last century, a horse shied, frightened by something invisible to the rider who was thrown and killed.

The phantom coach associated with Roos Hall, on the outskirts of Beccles, has already been mentioned in Chapter 2. Roos, sometimes called Rose Hall, is a moated red-brick Tudor manor house dating back to *c*. 1583. Apart from the grounds, haunted by a phantom coach with a headless groom, the house itself has a haunted bedroom, where according to Anthony D. Hippisley Coxe, (*Haunted Britain*, 1973) the Devil's footmarks could be seen inside a wardrobe. An ancient oak tree stands in the park, and it was in former times used as a gibbet. Ghosts of those who were hanged there haunt the site, and, if you walk around the tree six times, you can summon the Devil to appear. This is similar to the Bungay Druid Stone tradition described in Chapter 1.

While on the subject of phantom coaches and horses, the headless rider who appears at Icklingham, not far from Mildenhall, should be mentioned. He gallops on horseback over the water meadows at Temple Bridge, but sometimes it's only the sound of the horse's hooves that can be heard. Also, at Icklingham is a mound known as Deadman's Grave, where a ghostly horseman is buried. It's thought that he was a highwayman, perhaps buried near the scenes of his crime, and his spirit remains restless because he was denied a Christian burial. Horses rear up in fright as they near the spot, and cattle, and dogs, too, show signs of fear if they wander past the mound.

Westwood Lodge, once a Tudor manor house, stands on farmlands just outside Blythburgh. In the 1960's, Mrs Brown, the farmer's wife, recalled that she had heard ghostly footsteps pacing up and down on the first floor, one of the oldest parts of the building. She usually heard them around mid-day. A local man, who had lived with his mother in rooms above the dairy at the farm, remembered seeing the ghost of a woman, wearing a silk gown coming out of the study in the farmhouse.

The story of a lady wearing a silk dress, or a long silver dress, persisted, and in October 1972, three policemen decided to sit in the house after dark to see if they could witness any manifestations. By that time Mrs Brown had died, and the house was described in 1973 as sad, and sinister, and no more than a 'grim shell', so it was probably unoccupied – other than by the ghost, that is. They heard strange sounds, and experienced a chilly change of temperature, but didn't actually see any sign of a ghost, even though the son of the local gamekeeper claimed to have seen the 'Grey Lady', only a few nights before the policemen's visit.

Bealings House at Great Bealings, is between Woodbridge and Ipswich. In 1834, between 2 February and 27 March, all the servants bells in the house started to ring frequently, and without human aid. No explanation has ever been given. The continuous bell-ringing was experienced by Major Edward Moor, and he wrote an account of the strange occurrence in the *Ipswich Journal*, sometime after the event.

The house is also haunted by the ghost of a little old lady, dressed in grey, who has been seen sliding silently in and out of the powder-closet off one of the bedrooms. The owner of the house in *c.* 1950 told Alasdair Alpin Macgregor that he had seen her several times, and the author recorded his account in the Sphere magazine in 1951.

Waveney Cottage stands on the banks of the River Waveney, near Outney Common in Bungay. It was previously known as Outney Cottage, and dates back to the sixteenth century, one of few properties to survive the Great Fire of 1688, because it stands some distance from the town centre.

The present owners, Martin and Pauline Evans, bought the property about ten years ago. About six months after they moved in, Martin was working in the doorway of one of the outbuildings facing the front cobbled courtyard, when he looked up, and saw a tall woman entering the garden. She was dressed in Victorian costume, a poke bonnet, and a long, grey full-skirted dress, and carrying a basket. As she approached the front door, she bowed her head, as if stooping before entering.

Martin hurried down the drive to enquire who the visitor might be, but when he reached the door, it was firmly shut, and nobody in the house had seen or heard anybody knock or enter. Since that date, she has never been seen again.

Who could the ghostly visitor be? Perhaps a previous occupant of the property. In the late eighteenth and nineteenth century it was owned by the Scott family. Samuel Scott who also owned Scott House (formerly Bridge House) a bit closer to the town, was a prosperous fellmonger, dealing in animal skins, mainly sheep fleeces. He died in 1825, and the property passed to his son, also called Samuel. He had a twin-sister, Charlotte, who was crippled as the result of a riding-accident. Could she be the mysterious ghostly visitor? But no, she would never have been able to manage the steps in such a stately manner.

46. Waveney Cottage, Bungay.

The only other known likely candidate is Hannah Butcher, who also occupied the property as a kind of 'lady's companion'. In August 1853, Dr Hood, a cousin of Samuel Scott visited Bungay, and stayed at Waveney Cottage. He brought with him his son Charles Hood, who was the Lord Chancellor's Visitor in Lunacy for the Bethlem Hospital in London. On the arrival of these gentlemen, Hannah moved out to stay in lodgings in the town. Apparently, she did not get on with Dr Hood, and Martin surmises that it may be she whom he saw, calling to enquire whether the bad man from Bedlam had finally gone!

The unsettling thing about ghosts is that you never know if, or when they may appear again. A sudden rustling sound on the cobbles – a shadow falling on the path – some faintly muttered words. A trick of the wind, or has the ghostly lady returned?

No. 40, Earsham Street in Bungay has been a shop since the Victorian period. In the 1970s it was occupied by a couple selling a variety of decorative household items. Not long after they moved in they were disturbed by the sound of footsteps moving up and down the staircase outside their bedroom at night. At first they thought it might be one of their daughters returning late from a night out, but when they checked they were all sleeping peacefully in their beds. They never saw the ghost, and although the footsteps were disturbing, they never actually felt that the ghostly activity was threatening.

Sometime later they had renovation work done on the main chimney breast of the property, and after that, the midnight pit-pattering of footsteps ceased.

In the mediaeval period, and for centuries afterwards, it was believed that evil spirits would creep into a property through any available space, with chimneys being an obvious method of entry. To keep them away, objects such as witch-bottles, filled with human hair, nails, and urine were either placed in chimney niches, or sealed up behind the bricks of the hearth. These and other 'good luck' objects such as shoes, and mummified cats, have been found in several old houses throughout Suffolk, and, as mentioned earlier, there is an interesting collection of them on display in Moyses' Hall Museum in Bury St Edmunds.

So it may be that by interfering with the chimney and hearth area, the ghost of No. 40 was either pacified, and felt no further need to 'haunt', or else was frightened away. Hopefully he, or she, now rests in peace at last in the local churchyard.

One of the most extraordinary Suffolk ghost stories relates, not to a disappearing phantom figure, but a phantom house. In 1926, a teacher, Ruth Wynne, took her pupil, a fourteen-year-old girl, for a walk from Rougham Green, across the fields to Bradfield St George. Miss Wynne was a newcomer to the region, as her father had recently been appointed the Vicar of the Rougham parish, and she was keen to explore the area.

Following the path along the fields, they came to a park gate, where, peering through the wrought-iron gate, they could see a handsome Georgian house standing amidst spacious grounds. They admired it, wondered who might own it, and then continued on their way. On returning home, they each wrote a description of what they had seen on their walk, including the house.

A few weeks later, they took the same route, but coming to the place where they had seen the house they were amazed to see no sign of it there – no iron-gates, no park, – Nothing! When they returned home they made enquiries, but none of the locals knew of the existence of such a property – as far as they knew, it had never been anything other than an empty field.

However, it was subsequently revealed that in 1860, Robert Palfrey was thatching a haystack in a field in the Kingshall Street area, near where the two women had seen the mysterious house. He heard a sudden 'Swoosh-sh', and on looking down from his ladder, saw a large red-brick, double-fronted house behind an ornate wrought-iron gate, where, before there had been nothing but an empty field. It then disappeared. His great grandson, James Cobbold, in June, 1912, was driving along Kingshall Street in his horse and cart, when he also saw the phantom property. His account was published in *Amateur Gardening*, in December 1975.

If the house could be seen, during the day, on three widely separated occasions, by three different people, it must surely have been more than a trick of the light. That field should be regularly visited by those with the gift of psychic vision to see whether the mysterious house re-appears.

9

TERRIFYING TAVERNS

Is the Three Tuns in Bungay the most haunted pub in Britain? It's said to be haunted by as many as twenty different ghosts, although not necessarily all at the same time, otherwise visitors to the pub might find the atmosphere rather too crowded and unpleasant and take their custom elsewhere. Some appear at certain times, then disappear for a while, others take their place, then also disappear and pop back again later, just to be as unexpectedly terrifying as possible. Because for the ghost, the surprise appearance at the creaking door, in the glimmering moonlight, or hanging by a rope from the ceiling is essential. If you become too familiar, nobody will take you seriously and you loose a lot of 'street-cred' in the spirit world where every phantom is jostling for the role of spookiest spectre on the block, a bit like being a student at a drama school. In fact, one particular haunter of the Tuns has become a bit too regular in his appearances with the result that he was getting teased or ignored: more of him later.

The Tuns is one of Bungay's most ancient buildings, and it has even been suggested that the thick flint and stone-walled cellars may have originally formed part of Hugh Bigod's castle, just across the road, and built in the twelfth century. The upper part of the building was substantially damaged during the Great Fire of 1688, and it was later renovated in Georgian style.

It became a coaching inn, and fashionable resort for the local gentry in the eighteenth century, when a banqueting hall and Assembly Rooms were built on the first floor. Parson James Woodforde stayed at the inn in 1788, and comments in his diary on the fish and leg of mutton he enjoyed there.

The recorded ghostly hauntings date back to the sixteenth century, before the Great Fire. The earliest story relates to Lizzie Bowlynge a servant girl at the Tuns. In 1589, she was discovered stealing a quart jug of ale from the cellars, and, as punishment she was chained to the cellar wall and starved to death. A plaque records her plight.

She is one of the ghosts who continues to pervade the cellar area. The pub is currently under new management with renovations in the cellar area, so it will be interesting to see whether Lizzie and her fellow phantoms are scared off or become even more keen to scare others!

The character who features most often in stories is Rex Bacon, or Bocon. He was the eighteen-year-old son of a local clergyman at Mettingham, and got into trouble for stealing money from the church collections box. It's said that he hid the money in the inn. Later, he discovered that his wife was having an affair with another man, and, when

47. The Three Tuns, and King's Head, Market Place, Bungay.

he discovered them in bed together at the Tuns, he killed them both, and then hanged himself from a beam on the landing staircase in 1682.

The staircase has long been considered one of the most haunted parts of the building, where the ghost of Rex Bacon continues to linger, still hot with fury about his wife's infidelity and that she was the cause of his suicide. The rooms near the landing are often noisy at night with unexplained opening and shutting of windows, furniture being moved around, and mysterious voices. The manageress at the inn in the 1960's, Lucy Leggett, used to see Rex so frequently, that she became quite familiar with him, teasing him and calling him 'Charlie Boy'. But he retaliated on one occasion by giving her a push from behind, causing her to topple down the stairs, but fortunately she wasn't hurt.

Malcolm Bedingfield, who has lived in the town all his life, recalls other strange stories connected with the building. A couple staying there put their young child to bed in their guest room, leaving it to sleep while they went downstairs for an evening meal. They were not gone very long. When they returned, they were shocked to discover that every item of furniture in the room had been re-arranged, a task that would have taken two men a good deal of time to complete. Fortunately, their child was still sleeping apparently undisturbed by the disruption.

On another occasion, a young couple were occupying the same room. They decided to have their meal upstairs, in order to be alone. The woman was carrying the loaded tray upstairs, and her boyfriend went ahead to open the door for her. As she passed over the threshold, some invisible force hit the tray, knocking it out of her hand, so the food and drink was sent flying all over the room. The man thought she had tripped,

48. Rex Bacon hanging on the staircase of the Three Tuns, Bungay.

49. The staircase at the Three Tuns, Bungay.

and helped to clear up the mess. They then went downstairs to get a replacement meal, and just as she was carefully crossing the threshold to make sure the accident wasn't repeated, the tray was again knocked out of her hand and the food and drink spilled everywhere.

Both the couples, and Malcolm, attributed these happenings to poltergeist activity, which is certainly possible, but it could have been the playful ghost of Rex up to his old tricks again.

Rex seems to have been particularly active in the late 1960's and reports were featured in the *Beccles & Bungay Journal* of 4 July 1969. Mervyn Blakeway, of Beccles, and assistant manager at the Tuns, happened to have been living alone there a few years earlier, and described his experiences to the local journalist. He says he never actually saw any ghosts, but he could feel a 'presence' in certain rooms, and the window in his bedroom would on occasions open and close in an unexplained manner.

One particular window in the room would always be closed in the morning if I left it open on going to bed, and would always be open if I left it closed. On another occasion a different window facing from my room into a corridor slammed with such force that it must have been pushed.

Mervyn was at first disturbed and frightened by the building's 'dark interior', but as he became more used to being there he became accustomed to Rex Bacon's presence, and decided to challenge him by cheerfully calling 'Goodnight, Rex', on going to bed, and 'Come on, Rex, let me see you', when he climbed the stairs in the dark to the landing where the youth had hanged himself.

He mentions that Lucy Leggett the hotel manageress at the time was something of a psychic, and saw Rex four or five times. She described him as very young looking, with a happy playful expression on his face. 'Once, when with me going up the stairs, she said Look! There he is! But I couldn't see anything'.

Most of the information discovered about Rex resulted from some séances that Lucy Leggett held in the building. She, together with Mervyn Blakeway, Brian Prime the Tuns proprietor, and some regular customers, sat around a table on which the letters of the alphabet were arranged in a circle. A bottle was placed on the table, and as they sat in silence and trepidation, and tension around the table increased, Lucy summoned the ghost to appear. Slowly the bottle began to move, and it spelt out the answers to the questions she asked. In this way they gradually learned that the ghost's name was Rex Bacon or Bocon (it seems that he had Dutch or Flemish relatives so could have been a foreign name), and the details about his theft from Mettingham church, his wife's infidelity, his suicide, and that he had been haunting the hotel ever since due to his troubled and remorseful spirit.

Testimony to the haunting of this particular ghost comes from an unlikely source. About five years ago a new manager was appointed to run the bar at the Tuns, and he often brought his little son into the building with him. On one occasion as father and son were walking towards the staircase, the little boy suddenly pointed up towards the landing and asked: 'Daddy! What's that man doing hanging there?'

His father could hardly believe what he had heard the little boy say. He knew about the traditional tale of Rex's suicide, but of course he had never repeated it to his son, and yet it seemed the child could actually see the dead body hanging from the beam on the end of a rope. He quickly hurried him away, and made a joke about shadows playing strange tricks of light.

Children with their purity and innocence are often considered sensitive to sights and sounds that adults are less likely to experience, and so it does seem that in this case, he too picked up on a ghastly episode in the Tuns that had occurred more than three hundred years earlier.

Hearing this story it's difficult for even the sceptical to deny that there must be something spooky there.

Leslie Beckett, a hairdresser with his premises in Broad Street, opposite the Three Tuns, was another of the 'regulars' who had attended the séances. He told the *Beccles & Bungay Journal* reporter, that during one of the sessions, he saw a white, ghost-like figure in a corner of one of the hotel's rooms. Later, he discovered that the point at which the ghost had disappeared had originally contained a door which had later been sealed up. He added: 'There is one particular spot in the hotel which always makes me go cold, and I am not afraid to admit that I would not care to spend a night on my own there'. He was not prepared to admit where the 'cold' spot was in the building. Mr Beckett said he had known about the Rex Bacon ghost before the séances, whereas Mervyn Blakeway only found out about him during the sessions.

Although the Tuns' staff had been pleased with the results of their séance, the ghostly disturbances continued to be regular and troublesome. The proprietor, Brian Prime decided that action must be taken to calm things down. Tales about ghostly hauntings circulating in the town and local press might encourage a few new customers, but on the other hand it could put off large numbers of potential clients who, when they booked into a hotel, wished for a peaceful night's sleep.

He therefore invited a well known clergyman who specialised in psychic phenomena, Canon J.D. Pearce-Higgins, to perform a service of exorcism to release the troubled spirits from the building. The Canon was Vice-Provost of Southwark Cathedral, and vice-chairman of the Churches Fellowship for Psychical and Spiritual Studies. Having investigated the situation at the Tuns, he decided against a service of exorcism, and instead, held a Requiem Mass. He explained:

A service of exorcism is applicable only to demons and devils, if they exist, whereas happenings such as have occurred here in this hotel are caused by earth-bound humans who do not know they are dead. They are lost souls, and the Requiem Mass is to pray for their release and enlightenment.

The Canon concluded his work at the hotel by 'sealing' the entrance doors with sprinklings of holy water and making the sign of the cross over them, to prevent ghosts from re-entering.

However, the ghosts of Rex and the others didn't seem at all impressed by the Canon's intervention, and continued to carry on in the same way as before. BBC TV became interested and sent a journalist along to investigate, and it was agreed that a session with a well-known London medium, Donald Page, would be arranged, to see what he could discover.

For this event, twelve people gathered at the Tuns, including the BBC representative, Lucy Leggett, some of the regulars involved with her previous séance, and Canon Pearce- Higgins was also invited back to attend. Dr Hugh Cane, the local GP was also invited and he recorded what happened in a manuscript now in Bungay Museum.

The Canon told Dr Cane that the Tuns was crowded with a lot of troubled spirits, and one of them with whom he had been able to get in touch had a French sounding name, and had lived in Bungay Castle during the sixteenth century. The doctor retorted that this was very unlikely because the castle was in a ruined condition by that date. The Canon replied that he was not surprised, because 'statements made by spirits are often very unreliable'.

In fact, Dr Cane's dismissal of the suggestion may have been misleading. Although the Castle was in a ruinous state by the fourteenth century, it seems that it may have been rebuilt in the Tudor period, and therefore could have been occupied at that time. Also, the Bigod family who built the Castle, were of French origin having come over from Normandy in 1066 with William the Conqueror. And, as has already been described, there are ghosts at the Castle, which is not many yards distant from the Three Tuns.

Donald Page proceeded to conduct a séance that same evening at 11 p.m. but he was unable to reveal any more information about the ghostly goings-on at the Tuns. Dr Cane observed that he had been taking brandy before the séance started and appeared to be drunk, so perhaps spirits such as ghosts are antagonistic to those who have been taking 'spirits' and refuse to have anything to do with them. Mr Page also tried to investigate information about those seated around the table, but much of what he revealed seemed to be inaccurate, and Dr Cane concluded that he was a bit of a fraud. Or maybe it was the overdose of 'spirits' that contributed to his lack of accuracy.

The local journalist proceeded to investigate the authenticity of 'Rex Bacon's' revelations, and visited All Saints church at Mettingham to ascertain whether he could have been the son of the incumbent there in the late seventeenth century. The evidence was inconclusive. He discovered that the Reverend John Hacon, a name not very different from 'Bacon' had been vicar from 1694 to 1731, and a century earlier, the Reverend Thomas Bacon had been vicar from 1520 to 1539. The resident vicar, the Reverend J.B. Skelhorn, told the journalist that he had not heard the stories about the Three Tuns ghosts. They looked through the relevant pages of the seventeenth century parish registers, but the faded writing and scrawly handwriting made most of the entries illegible.

The final words on the subject reported in the Journal of July 1969, were from Mervyn Blakeway and Brian Prime. Mervyn concluded by saying that he had found the ghost of Rex Bacon to be of a friendly and protective disposition, and was disappointed that Mr Prime should want to exorcise him. Brian stated that he was hesitant about being interviewed because many people would treat the matter as a joke and he did not wish to be made 'the laughing stock of Bungay'. He added:

I have never been particularly bothered about the ghosts in any case. I invited the Canon because the strange happenings here fascinated rather than alarmed me. I just wanted to know what was going on.

And many local people today are STILL fascinated to know what is going on in the haunted Three Tuns.

Another frequently told tale concerns a highwayman, Tom Hardy. He often used the pub as his headquarters when he was perpetrating his crimes in the area, riding out into the countryside, and waylaying coach and horses after dark, by crying 'Stand and deliver', and brandishing a brace of pistols.

It's possible he was either an accomplice, or at least an associate, of Britain's most notorious highwayman, Dick Turpin. Turpin's main territory for crime, which included house-breaking and cattle-stealing, as well as robbery on the highways, was in London, but he also visited other parts of the country with his confederate Tom King. In 1739, the two men took a ride from London, and alighted for refreshment in Bungay on Market Day. They may have intended to meet up with Tom Hardy at the Tuns nearby. However, they happened to observe two pretty young women receiving payment for some sacks of corn which they had just sold at the old Corn Cross.

Turpin determined to steal the money from them, although his partner argued that it was a shame to steal from two such pretty, innocent creatures. But Turpin was nothing more than a vicious thug, and having forced the girls to hand over the cash he and Tom King then quickly raced off into the countryside before the girls could summon aid.

Shortly after this episode, Turpin was arrested for horse-stealing, and hanged on the gallows at York. It seems that the robbery of the two girls in Bungay was one of the last of his crimes, and they probably never got their money back.

Tom Hardy, as far as we know, was not involved in that particular crime, but he perpetrated many others in the area, and he too, was eventually caught, convicted and hanged. As a regular customer at the Tuns, he returned to haunt the place, and can still be seen at various times, in his eighteenth century clothing and tricorn hat. It would make a nice story if it could be claimed that he returns to haunt Bungay as penitence for assisting Dick Turpin with the robbery of the two pretty girls; but unfortunately there is no information to support it. If the stones of Old Bungay could speak, what tales they could tell!

A gruesome event took place in the Tuns in February, 1787, when the murdered body of Henry Scarle, was laid out in the upstairs Assembly Room for public display.

Henry Scarle was a young man employed by Mathias Kerrison, a wealthy businessman who owned the Bungay Staithe navigation on the River Waveney. Scarle's job was to look after the vessels transporting corn and other goods at Whitacre Burgh. He began to notice that some of the goods were being stolen, and kept watch one night to see if he could detect the thieves. He soon spotted two men, William Hawke, of Beccles, and Thomas Mayhew of Bungay who stealthily approached, and began loading the corn from a wherry to carry away. Scarle slipped away undetected, and reported the thieves to his master. However, before they could be caught and detained, they heard that Scarle had informed against them, and boarding the vessel where he was working on the night of 10 February, they bludgeoned him to death, and left his body floating in the river.

They then lay low in the neighbourhood, waiting for the opportunity to get away. A few days later, as they were attempting to escape to London, they were apprehended at Botesdale by some vigilantes employed by the Bungay Association. They were tried and convicted of Scarle's murder at the Norwich Assizes, and hanged on Castle Hill in the city in March of the same year.

It seems that it was Matthias Kerrison's idea to have his murdered employee's body displayed in the Three Tuns. He had made a fortune out of his local business interests, and now saw an opportunity to profit from the boy's death. The public were admitted to view Scarle's body for a fee of a penny a time, and it must have made a gruesome spectacle, having been beaten in the most brutal manner, and then drowned. Kerrison could claim that he only wished to organise the event out of respect, and as a warning that those who, like Hawke and Mayhew, committed such terrible crimes could expect to be hanged on the gallows. But several of the spectators muttered that the pennies Kerrison collected would more than pay for the boy's funeral and tombstone; and the beer provided for their refreshment was probably from Kerrison's own brewery. No wonder then, that he was to become Bungay's first self-made millionaire.

Scarle was eventually allowed to be buried in peace in Holy Trinity churchyard, not far from Bungay Staithe. His gravestone can still be seen there, and bears the following inscription:

To the Memory of Henry Scarle
Who was valued when alive,
And respected now dead,
Was cruelly murdered at Whitacre Burgh
On the 10th of February, 1787,
In the 23rd year of his age.
Honest and Industrious Men were never known
To commit such a horrid crime as this.

So does Henry Scarle's ghost still mingle with the others in the Three Tuns, aggrieved that he had been murdered when all that he was trying to do was protect his master's property? Or, even more aggrieved that he should have been put on display like a circus freak so his master could make a handsome profit?

Facing the Three Tuns across the street is the King's Head, another ancient coaching inn, dating back to Tudor times, and rebuilt after the Great Fire. It backs onto the Castle, and a flight of steps from the inn yard leads directly up to the Castle keep. It may be that some of the ghostly disturbances at the King's Head, are related to events from the dim and distant past at Hugh Bigod's castle.

In the original sixteenth century part of the house, one particular guest bedroom, Room two, on the first floor overlooking the rear yard towards the Castle, has a disturbing atmosphere. The current manager, Geoff Bryan says that he used to sleep in the room next door, when he first moved into the pub, and strange noises emanated from it. As soon as you enter the room it feels unnaturally cold, yet the room next door has a normal temperature. The door is on a deadlock, and sometimes, when the cleaners lock it, it mysteriously re-opens, or if opened, it mysteriously locks itself. Guests who have slept there have reported an oppressive atmosphere, and have woken in the night feeling a heavy tightness on their necks and chests, as if somebody was pressing hard against them. Another couple refused to sleep in the room because they felt as if somebody else was there with them.

To the rear of the original inn is a large building known as the Oddfellows Hall, built in the late nineteenth century. It has a ballroom on the first floor, and Geoff, and his staff, have always felt that it has a strange eerie atmosphere. On one occasion, a cleaner alone in the room felt as if a strange presence was there with her, and when she tried to leave down the stairs, it seemed as if this thing, or person, was trying to block her departure. On another occasion, Geoff was clearing up downstairs after an event, when he seemed to hear faint music coming from the ballroom, like the sound of Glenn Miller's Band. He mentioned it to a friend of his in the building and going upstairs they could both hear the music, but when they entered the room, there was no explanation as to where it could have come from. Other people have mentioned strange music relating to the 1940's and wonder whether it's connected with some incident that might have happened there during the Second World War, when dances were staged for soldiers and their girlfriends in the ballroom.

Geoff got so spooked by the funny goings on, that late one night, he issued a challenge to the unseen intruder: 'Come on then, I want to see who you are'. At that very moment he heard the sound of footsteps walking from the bar area towards him, but couldn't see anybody – the footsteps paused, as if somebody had stopped to stare at him, then walked a little way around him, and then stopped again. Geoff was so taken back that the 'ghost' had actually approached him, that he left the room as fast as he could. What might have happened if he'd stayed?

It seems that there must be something particularly appealing for ghosts in this part of the town, with the Castle, the King's Head, and the Three Tuns, all quite close together, and all haunted by a variety of strange spectres. St Mary's church, just across the road, with the Druid's or Devil's Stone in the churchyard, is on a major ley-line, and this may have some bearing on the spirit-charged atmosphere.

The King's Head at nearby Beccles is also a haunted hotel. A young woman, known as Matilda was a chambermaid there at the beginning of the eighteenth century. She fell in love with a groom, who also worked there. They became lovers, and soon, Matilda was pregnant with his child. Unwilling to face up to his responsibilities, the groom abandoned her. She was heartbroken, and knowing the stigma attached to being an unmarried mother at that time, felt that the only way out of her plight was suicide. But some say that the desperate Matilda, never quite left the hotel, and centuries later, her lonely spirit still wanders around the corridors, and through the rooms late at night, lamenting the loss of both her lover, and her unborn child.

The King's Head has now combined with a local brewery to market a beer commemorating this tragic love affair. Martin Grove is the present food and beverage manager for the hotel, and the beer is produced by Engel Fine Ales of Opa Hay's Brewery at nearby Aldeby. The beer is named 'Matilda's Revenge', although the exact nature of the 'revenge' remains a bit unclear. In any case it seems a novel way of commemorating a long time resident of the ancient inn, and the beer, which has a distinctive flavour of Boudica hops, is likely to cheer the spirits of the King's Head clients, even if it can't do much to assuage the tormented soul of poor Matilda. She is also commemorated in the regular summer 'Ghost Walks' organised in the town, and no doubt many will end the tour by sharing in 'Matilda's Revenge' at the end of the evening walk.

The Crown Hotel at Bildeston, not far from Long Melford, is associated with a number of hauntings. The building dates back to the fifteenth century, but the ghosts all seem to be of a later period, eighteenth or nineteenth centuries from the descriptions of the clothes they are wearing.

One is a woman wearing a grey dress. She was a maidservant, who haunts the courtyard area, and the stables, where she hanged herself. The reason is not explained

50. The Bull, at Long Melford.

but probably due to problems with her employment, like the maidservant at the Bungay Three Tuns, or an unhappy love affair.

There is also an old gentlemen wearing a tricorn hat, from the eighteenth or early nineteenth century when such headgear was fashionable. Two children appear from time to time, in ragged Victorian clothes and playing with a music-box. Customers in the bar may suddenly feel an icy cold clutch on their necks – jumping in alarm they look round – but there's nobody there! In one of the rooms a suicide occurred, and in another a woman was strangled. Strange sounds, footsteps and wailings occur at night. Hardly a good advertisement for the business, so no details will be added. Just go along and enjoy a drink and a meal, and if anything 'extra' is served up, at least you'll have a jolly good story to tell your friends afterwards. That is, if you survive to tell the tale.

The Bull at Long Melford dates back to the sixteenth century or earlier. In 1648, a yeoman farmer, Richard Everard, was stabbed there during a quarrel with Roger Greene. The body was laid out in the hotel parlour, but by the following morning it had vanished, nobody knows why or where. It was therefore rumoured that the coffin buried in the churchyard never contained a body. Both the criminal and the victim are said to haunt the rooms of the Bull.

111

51. The Angel, at Lavenham.

52. Angel hanging sign.

The sounds of howling phantom dogs are sometimes heard and there is poltergeist activity. On one occasion a number of dining-room chairs had been moved from their usual places, and arranged around the hearth, as if a group of people had drawn them together for a friendly chat. The pub has a great atmosphere, and many historic period details, so the ghosts add that extra little frisson of excitement that every old British inn needs.

At the Angel Inn in Lavenham, you are also stepping right back into the town's historic past for it obtained a licence for serving meat and alcohol in 1420. It's one of the architectural gems of a town of well-preserved half-timbered buildings, so an ideal place to quench your thirst after a wander around admiring a street centre which looks as if it's been specially constructed as a Hollywood film set. The Angel is haunted by a little old lady in an old-fashioned gown, said to be Mrs Goodhew, a former landlady. She's probably keeping an eye on the business and making sure that the ale is as good, and the benches as well-polished as when she was in charge. She seems to be a good tempered ghost, because a later pub manageress saw her admiring the Christmas tree on one occasion, and turned to smile when she realised that she was being stared at. If only all ghosts could be so pleasant.

53. The White Hart, Blythburgh.

The White Hart Inn at Blythburgh is haunted by a small elderly man dressed in monk's clothing. In earlier centuries the building had been used as an ecclesiastical court house, which explains the presence of a clerical figure, and the ruins of the ancient Blythburgh Priory are nearby. Joan Forman, in her book *Haunted East Anglia,* records that behind the bar of the pub is an oak door, from which a knocking has been heard as if the visitor was wearing a ring. She concludes that the prior from the nearby Priory would have worn an official ring denoting his office, so perhaps he is the monk-like intruder.

The figure was seen by the landlord and his wife in the 1960's on several occasions, and in 1967, three disasters occurred: a lorry crashed into the end wall of the building and the driver was killed; the pub was subsequently burgled, and later in the same year the building was damaged by fire. It is thought that the ghostly intruder was responsible and since these catastrophes he has been seen less often.

The former White Hart at Wickham Market is haunted by a woman dressed in a tunic made of sacking. She hangs around the bar area, and seems to be a different figure from that of Betty Price, who was a landlady at the inn in the eighteenth century and was tried and convicted of witchcraft, and subsequently executed. One of the guest bedrooms, No. fourteen is particularly spooky and visitors report disturbed nights after staying there.

The premises closed as an inn towards the end of the last century, and are now used as shops, offices and a flat.

Other pubs worth mentioning are the Horse & Groom at Melton, haunted by a cat, perhaps because cats were sometimes bricked up in the walls of old houses to protect the inmates from evil spirits. At the Swan in Lavenham, Room fifteen is haunted by an under house-keeper who hanged herself out of distress and jealousy when a colleague was promoted above her.

Bury St Edmund's Nutshell is the haunt of a small boy with a miserable face. He can be seen standing at the end of the bar, and locals joke that he would have been chased out years ago as an underage drinker, if the police were doing their job properly. Actually it seems he was probably murdered on the premises, so he has no reason to look cheerful. Another ghostly visitor is a monk, who also shouldn't be hanging around in a bar: but creepy monks are two a penny in Bury, where the Abbey of St Edmund was situated in the mediaeval period, and perhaps the Nutshell is on the site of a building formerly connected with the abbey.

A mummified cat and a decidedly spooky atmosphere all contribute to the attractions of the neat little Nutshell. Locals who drink there regularly must now feature in thousands of photos taken by American and Japanese tourists all eager to return home with proof that they've had a drink in Britain's tiniest tavern.

In the same street as the Nutshell is Cupola House, with an elegant Georgian façade. It has been haunted by a Grey Lady for several centuries, and she is also rumoured to float along the web of underground cellars and secret passages with which, the local gossips tell us, the town centre is honey-combed.

And so this book concludes its accounts of the many and varied ghosts that haunt Suffolk. Despite the often grim and sordid tales that are included here, the ghosts themselves are rather an endearing and pathetic array of creatures. They often suffered much turmoil in their lives, and the reason why many of them continue to haunt the area today is because they wish, like Coleridge's Ancient Mariner, to confess their sins, and

54. The Swan at Lavenham.

their griefs, and be understood. Only in this way can they feel free from the burden of guilt that wracks them, and lie down to sleep at last in their graves in the serene Suffolk countryside.

We feel kinship with them, because we can sympathise with their plights – the emotions and fears which drove them to their desperate ends, resulting in murder, or suicide, or the hangman's rope: and sympathy for their victims too. They were all frail humans like us. And, who knows? – among the many friends and acquaintances we see around us today, may be some who will also be doomed to haunt the earth long after they have been buried in their graves.

LIST OF ILLUSTRATIONS

1. Scribbly Skull. Drawing by Mike Tingle.
2. Moyse's Hall Museum, courtesy of St Edmundsbury Council museums.
3. St Lawrence's Church, Ilketshall, beside the Roman road, Stone Street. Courtesy of Martin Evans.
4. Roman god, on the porch of St Lawrence's church, Ilketshall. Courtesy of Martin Evans.
5. Roman road with advancing soldiers. Drawing by Mike Tingle.
6. Druid Stone, St Mary's Church, Bungay. Courtesy of Martin Evans.
7. Roman and Saxon 'Ghosts' return to haunt the ancient town of Bungay. Courtesy of Frank Honeywood Collection, Bungay Museum.
8. Bungay Castle. Engraving by T. Higham, 1817, courtesy of Bungay Museum.
9. Phantom horses. Drawing by Mike Tingle.
10. Framlingham Castle. Courtesy of Martin Evans.
11. 'Doom' detail from the fifteenth century panel painting in Wenhaston Church. Courtesy of Martin Evans.
12. St Mary's Church and Priory, Bungay. Engraving by Henry Davy, c. 1816, courtesy of Bungay Museum.
13. Barsham Church.
14. Anne Boleyn, Courtesy of Jonathan Reeve JR995b66fp24 15001600.
15. The White Lady, Covehithe churchyard. Drawing by Mike Tingle.
16. The Black Dog of Bungay. Drawing by Mike Tingle.
17. The Black Dog in St Mary's Church. Woodcut illustration in the pamphlet *A Strange and Terrible Wunder*, reprinted by T & H. Rodd, 1826, courtesy of Bungay Museum.
18. St Mary's Church, Bungay. Courtesy of Martin Evans.
19. Blythburgh Church. Courtesy of Jasmine Lingwood.
20. Door of Blythburgh church with the scorched claw-marks of the Black Dog. Courtesy of Martin Evans.
21. Black Dog weathervane, Bungay Market Place. Courtesy of Frank Honeywood Collection, Bungay Museum.
22. Gargoyle, on the North wall of St Mary's church, designed to scare away evil spirits. Courtesy of Bungay Museum.
23. Lowestoft. Photo by Nick Catling, courtesy of Tourism dept. Waveney District Council.

24. The Galley-Trot. Drawing by Mike Tingle.
25. Leiston Church. Courtesy of Martin Evans.
26. 'Guardian Angel', Blythburgh churchyard, scaring away evil spirits from the church. Courtesy of Martin Evans.
27. The coast at Dunwich. Courtesy of Jasmine Lingwood.
28. Woods near Dunwich. Courtesy of Jasmine Lingwood.
29. Waiting for the Walberswick Ferry. Drawing by Mike Tingle.
30. Oulton Broad. Photo by Jon Gibbs, courtesy of Tourism dept. Waveney District Council.
31. Sutherland House, Southwold. Courtesy of Jasmine Lingwood.
32. Gun Hill, Southwold. Photo by Jon Gibbs, courtesy of Tourism dept. Waveney District Council.
33. Orford Castle. Courtesy of Martin Evans.
34. Freshwater Mermaid. Drawing by Mike Tingle.
35. Homersfield Bridge. Courtesy of Jasmine Lingwood.
36. Flixton Hall, engraving, by T. Higham, *c.* 1817. Courtesy of Frank Honeywood Collection, Bungay Museum.
37. The Gypsy's Grave, near Newmarket. Courtesy of Martin Evans.
38. Toby's Walks, Suffolk County Council Picnic site, Blythburgh. Courtesy of Martin Evans.
39. Toby's Walks, Information plaque, Suffolk County Council. Courtesy of Martin Evans.
40. Deadmen's Corner, Yoxford. Courtesy of Martin Evans.
41. Dead man hanging. Drawing by Mike Tingle.
42. Frederick Rolfe. Courtesy of Bungay Museum.
43. Lowestoft. Photo by Ian Dinmore, courtesy of Tourism dept. Waveney District Council.
44. The Farmer's Ghost. Drawing by Mike Tingle.
45. Roos Hall, near Beccles.
46. Waveney Cottage, Bungay. Courtesy of Martin Evans.
47. The Three Tuns, and King's Head, Market Place, Bungay. Courtesy of Frank Honeywood Collection, Bungay Museum.
48. Rex Bacon hanging on the staircase of the Three Tuns, Bungay. Drawing by Mike Tingle.
49. The staircase at the Three Tuns, Bungay. Courtesy of Frank Honeywood Collection, Bungay Museum.
50. The Bull, at Long Melford. Courtesy of Martin Evans.
51. The Angel, at Lavenham. Courtesy of Martin Evans.
52. Angel hanging sign.
53. The White Hart, Blythburgh. Courtesy of Martin Evans.
54. The Swan at Lavenham. Courtesy of Martin Evans.

ACKNOWLEDGEMENTS

Grateful thanks to the following for providing photographs: Martin Evans, with whom I enjoyed two wonderful Spring mornings tootling around all the most picturesque villages of Suffolk; my sister, Jasmine Lingwood, for the photos of the Southwold and Dunwich areas: Darren Newman, Services Manager, Tourism and Events, Waveney District Council; Frank Honeywood for the photos now in the Bungay Museum collection; Professor Christopher Hand, Town Reeve of Bungay, for permitting the students' practise skeleton from Bungay Medical Centre, to be photographed for the front cover of the book; and especially Mike Tingle for his spooky and atmospheric ink drawings.

BIBLIOGRAPHY

The following books have provided the most useful sources of ghost stories for the Suffolk region, and have been extensively referred to in my own text.

The best, the most recent, and the most comprehensive book on the whole subject of British folk lore, is *The Lore of the Land*, by Jennifer Westwood and Jacqueline Simpson, Penguin Books, 2005. The same authors have also published *The Penguin Book of Ghosts*, 2008, which is basically a collection of all the most interesting supernatural tales extracted from the larger book. My only grouse is that my name as the author of *A Straunge & Terrible Wunder: the Story of the Black Dog of Bungay*, has been mis-spelt as Reede, instead of Reeve, in both volumes.

Other useful works include:

Haunted East Anglia, by Joan Forman, Fontana Books, 1976.

The Folklore of East Anglia, by Enid Porter, Batsford, 1974.

County Folklore: Printed Extracts, No. 2, Suffolk. Collected and edited by the Lady Eveline Camilla Gurdon, originally published by the Folklore Society, 1893; reprinted facsimile edition, 1997.

Ghosts of Suffolk, by Betty Puttick, Countryside Books, 1998.

The Ghost Book: Strange Hauntings in Britain. Alasdair Alpin MacGregor, 1955.

Haunted Britain. Antony D. Hippisley Coxe, Pan Books, 1975.

NOTES

Introduction: The quotation is from Samuel Taylor Coleridge's *The Rime of the Ancient Mariner*, part VI.

Chapter 1

The St Edmund legends are told in *Norfolk & Suffolk*, M.R. James, p. 18.

Chapter 2

Bigod hauntings – *In the Footsteps of Borrow and FitzGerald*, Morley Adams, 1914.
Bungay Castle, Elizabeth Bonhote, ed. Curt Herr, Zittaw Press, 2006. Introduction, p. 31.

Chapter 3

Katherine de Montacute – *Old Bungay*, Ethel Mann, 1934 reprinted by Morrow & Co., 1984.
Thomas Seckford – *The Companion Guide to East Anglia*, John Seymour, Collins, 1970.

Chapter 4

Much of the material concerning the Black Dog, and Black Shuck, in this and the succeeding chapter, is derived from my book: *A Straunge & Terrible Wunder: The Story of the Black Dog of Bungay*, pub. Morrow & Co., 1988, and now out of print.
The Churchwardens Registers for St Mary's Parish, Bungay are housed in the Lowestoft Library & Record Office, Suffolk.
Pamphlet, '*A Straunge & Terrible Wunder*', is in the British Library, and there is a facsimile in Bungay Museum.

Diabolical dog at Messina: *Dog*, Patricia Dale-Green, 1966.
Communion Rails: *Guide to Holy Trinity Church, Bungay*, Canon Frank Fuller, 1985.

Chapter 5

Winfarthing Black Dog – reported in the *Norwich Mercury*, 28 January 1944, and
included in *Black Shuck*, by Ivan Bunn, in the periodical *Lantern,* 1977. His article
is also the source for other interesting material in this chapter, including the Barnby
encounter, and the man working near Blythburgh church.
Halesworth witches – *Witchcraft and Demonism*, C.L. L'Estrange, 1933.
Smuggling activities in Norfolk and Suffolk: *Smugglers All: Centuries of Norfolk
Smuggling*, Kenneth Hipper, The Lark Press, 2001.

Chapter 6

The fascinating story of the wherry *Mayfly* is told *in Ghosts of the Broads*, by Dr
Charles Sampson, 1931, and included in *Ghosts of Suffolk* by Betty Puttick.
Bell ringing at the Harbour Inn, Southwold; *Haunted Southwold*, by Alasdair Alpin
MacGregor, East Anglian Magazine, Feb. 1961.
Description of the Orford merman, by Ralph of Coggeshall, is included in *Castles of
Suffolk*, by Peter Tryon, 2004.

Chapter 7

North Quay, Lowestoft murder: *Tales and Tall Stories*, Jack Rose, 1992.

Chapter 8

Information concerning the FitzGerald family is derived from *By Friends Possessed: A
Life of Edward FitzGerald*. Robert Bernard Martin, Faber, 1985.

Chapter 9

Haunted Taverns, by Donald Stuart, Tempus Books, 2007, has provided some useful
details for this chapter.

Also available from Amberley Publishing

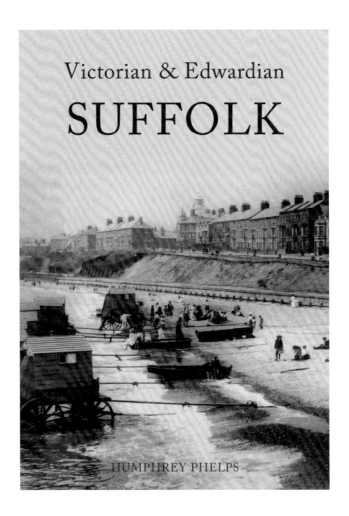

£14.99 Paperback
150 photographs
144 pages
978-1-84868-029-6

Available from all good bookshops or to order direct
please call **01285–760–030**